SHRINK RAP

Finding Rhyme and Reason in
Our Lives and Relationships

NEAL MAYERSON, PHD

Thanks to Bethany Kelly of Publishing Partner for production support
and publishing guidance and Pam Saeks of Boom for organizational
and marketing insights and for thinking of the book title.

Printed and bound in the United States of America
ISBN: 978-0-578-73893-2

DEDICATION

"As the sun rises, may we soar."
Loving you forever and then beyond.

And to my mother, who always embraced my softer
side and indulged my early philosophical curiosities
with loving patience.

And to Jay, my brother in poetry/spirit.

TABLE OF CONTENTS

INTRODUCTION

My life is punctuated with moments of condensed clarity of meaning. Each of these moments is inevitably fleeting, like a shooting star, and beyond the boundaries of thought. No matter, they ring true and pure. The experience can be like gazing through crystal clear ocean water at objects below that are distorted by currents and refractions of light. Despite not being *seen* clearly, the presence of the object is *known* clearly. Such moments capture my attention. I look closer. My left brain wrestles to translate the truth into thought, as my right brain basks in awe. Poetic thought for me has been the vehicle for bringing both sides together and is something I have been doing since I was 16 years old.

At some point along the way I became enamored of haiku poetry.

An old pond—
The sound
Of a diving frog.

Matsuo Basho was one of the Japanese masters of this art form and the author of the above poem. In this poem he puts you in the moment. With these few words, I find myself sitting in Nature, feeling tranquil, and then hearing that special sound of a frog perfectly breaking the surface of the water, which crystallizes the moment. The awe of the experience is amplified. The choice of the word "old" strategically elaborates on the setting—just a single word. My mind wanders to what the frog was doing on the land and what it is transitioning to do in the water. And, my mind stretches to the point in evolution when amphibians emerged, and the idea that humans might have evolved from the sea. I then return to the contemplative state, sitting by the water. Basho's selected few words activate and enliven my mind, heart, and imagination.

So, as I considered a form of poetic thought for encapsulating crystallized moments of truth and fascination, I was inspired by haiku. However, my personality is such that I am turned off by writing in accordance with the rules of haiku. I am, however, able to live with one primary rule, namely limiting myself to four lines. My brother referred to this form as "myku," as it was defined by *my* rules while being inspired by the aesthetics of haiku.

Over the years I have been writing in this form. The collection herein represents work drawn from experiences as a psychotherapist, a new father, a man in love and marriage, and generally a "people watcher." Every "myku" poem is based on perfect moments when I experienced the clarity of being in the presence of deep Truth. I was compelled in each case to capture the moment for my own scrapbook.

In time, across many conversations with my dear friend Jay, I noted that it was not uncommon for either of us to refer to one of these mykus as capturing the essence of what we were talking about in the moment. At other times, interesting conversations emerged from a myku that one of us had written, or conversations inspired a new myku from one or both of us. This brought me to revisiting my mykus and reflecting on them after the fact of their creation. These reflections, which accompany the mykus in this collection, are not meant to explain the meaning embedded in the original perfect moment. One does not explain the magic of a shooting star to a co-witness. Each person experiences it in their own way, and the experience evokes different thoughts. Moments like these are experienced through the lenses the individual brings to the moment, and those lenses change with time. The reflections herein express how the poem hit me at the moment of reflection. Readers will experience the poems through their own lenses. I certainly hope my reflections do not rob readers of their own reactions and interpretations.

My decision to publish what has been up until now my personal scrapbook of meaningful moments rests on the following. First, the following quote attributed to the philosopher/writer Émile Zola hit me as a directive from the Universe:

"If you ask me what I came to do in this world, I, an artist, will answer you: I am here to live out loud."

Second, with age I developed a better appreciation of the value added to my life by various artists and writers making their creations available to others ... to me. I am glad they did so, and it moved me to put my two cents into the world for whatever reader somewhere in the world at some time might value it. And, finally, just prior to my father passing, he suggested to me that I write more and put it out for others. So, here you go. I hope you find value. I hope you might share some mykus with others and that they might spark connective conversation.

PART ONE

The Human Condition

Gravity

Gravity is a fact of my life,
I jump and smile ... it holds on tight.
But some seem to be more immune,
As if they're in a cartoon on the moon.

REFLECTION ON "GRAVITY"

I am a serious person. There are substantive values about which I care deeply—honor, integrity, altruism, humanism, helping others, and improving the world as I'm able. And there's my empathy for people in pain and my personal existential angst. And so on and so on. Much of my life is spent in serious pursuits. Lightness of being is not my baseline state of being. This is a fact of my life. As basic as gravity is in the physical world, the gravity of serious things in life occupies my psychological world.

I used to look around at others who seemed to be unconcerned with such things and be struck by how different we were. While I was trying to figure out how the world worked, they were planning parties. I was more reflective and inquisitive about being human, and they were more transactional and action oriented. While I was trying to dive below the surface of things, they seemed content splashing and playing on the surface. I used to be truly dumbfounded by these people. How do they do it? They seemed like cartoon characters from a different planet.

Now the contrast between me and "them" is less stark. I suspect as we all have grown older that I have become more like them and they have become more engaged with the seriousness of life. In any event, I still acknowledge that gravity is a fact of *my* life and that I am serious about living my life well.

Growing

There are dancers in this robot man,
Rising from some slumber land,
Aching to dance free.
They will not be kept still.

REFLECTION ON "GROWING"

Each of us has an essence—a True Self – that evolves as we grow. That True Self exists along with an Adapted Self which is comprised of those aspects of ourselves that have come to be as a result of adapting to social demands we encounter. For example, a young girl may be a tomboy at heart—loving to climb and dig and run and get dirty. Her parents may have a different view of what they want in their daughter—a prim and proper girl. She is small and completely dependent on their approval. They are large and in charge. They give her frilly dresses to wear, and tell her to speak in hushed tones, and discourage her from rough and tumble play. She acquiesces. She suppresses her tomboy and instead acts in accordance with her parents' wishes. What else can she do? To the degree she is aware of this compromise of True Self she experiences existential pain. More likely she is unaware of the compromise as it quickly submerges into her subconscious. Her playfulness goes underground. Her gregariousness gets choked. And, she begins her journey of disconnecting from her True Self and developing a discomfort in her own skin that she doesn't understand. Others can feel her disquietude when interacting with her.

I remember feeling these compromised parts in my early 20s. I wasn't sure what they were. When aspects of personality are separated out early on, one doesn't spend enough time wearing them to develop a very clear picture of what they look like and how they feel.

So, I felt "something" inside that was yearning for expression—but the vision of what was inside was nothing more than a vague presence. Like a person with a visual impairment, I saw a shadow, a presence of a face, but I couldn't make out any features. My psyche knew I had an opportunity for these submerged parts to come forward, and so it allowed awareness. I felt inevitability. It was happening. Like a buoy tethered underwater and then cut free, it was rising. It was not something I was controlling. I just felt the bubbles rising, and I felt effervescent. I was growing up.

From the moment of birth, our lives unfold as a dynamic tension between our natural tendencies and the way others want us to be. We are placed in another's arms and immediately their wants and needs begin colliding with our own. Who we become results from natural tendencies such as those encoded in our DNA and the environmental forces that mold our adaptations. For this reason the notion of a True Self is a difficult one to pin down. But, if we pay close attention, we can tell when we feel "out of our own skin" and when, alternatively, we feel comfortable and wholesome in our being. Many of us are on a lifelong journey of discovering our True Self and living it out fully.

Truthache

I have a truthache.
Numb me,
Yank it,
Give me my blanket.

REFLECTION ON "TRUTHACHE"

After many years as a psychotherapist, I came to the realization that so much of what I was observing was the tangled web of knots that develop as we keep denying reality to ourselves in order to make life easier at the moment. Let's take a single thread as an example. A partner in a relationship senses that things aren't going well in the relationship, but because he doesn't want to deal with it in the moment, he sets it aside *as if* everything is fine. The other partner also senses a disconnect happening, but instead decides to check it out by asking if everything is OK, to which the answer is "Yeah. Just fine." The seed of distrust is planted. Each person knows that it is not all OK between them; one is denying it and the other is left with nagging doubt as she wrestles with the little lie about there being nothing amiss. The distrust grows over time as each little lie to themselves and each other festers a growing distrust. Distrust then leads to accusations, some of which are accurate and some that are imaginary worries. Each person feels wrongly accused and mistreated, leading to defensiveness and resentment. Resentment explodes into anger. Anger causes misbehavior. To whatever extent there was something "wrong" at the beginning of this sequence, it has now grown by leaps and bounds along with a litany of transgressions, small and large. The distance between them is growing. Then, one partner's discontent grows to a point that they decide that if they are being accused of infidelity and can't get their spouse to trust them, they might as well actually seek comfort and pleasure with another person and at least enjoy the pleasures of what they are being accused of. Things are crumbling.. The writing goes on the wall, and eventually the relationship falls apart. Phew! Maybe, just maybe, all of this might have been prevented if at the outset they had just talked through the fact that they were missing each other as they both had become so busy with life's responsibilities.

The truths of problems, challenges, and uncertainties are too often easier to deny than to deal with. By and large I think we'd all be better off if we developed more grit to be able to face truths as they come up and deal with them, instead of creating lies that beget lies over and over to the point of becoming a big gnarled and knotty ball of twine that's nearly impossible to unravel. We paint ourselves into corners, where the only option seems to be a continuation of denying reality when it is difficult to handle. We grab our comforting blanket and pull it over our eyes as we run from our challenges. But, as the saying goes, "You can run but you can't hide."

The Gift

The gift you give
With sincerity,
Arouses commanded affection,
And I squeamishly acquiesce.

REFLECTION ON "THE GIFT"

I hate when social expectations lead to inauthenticity. For example, love is so precious as to be sacred to me, and as such should not be bandied about as a mere social convention. Signing "love" on letters and cards that are being sent to casual acquaintances or distant relatives has never felt "accurate" and true to me. Or, reciprocating an "I love you" after the same has been offered up to you seems to lack authenticity. Love is the most precious experience for humans—the ultimate toward which we strive. Therefore, in my mind, when someone pronounces their love, it is a serious matter. I, for one, want to know it's being offered with sincerity. It becomes cheapened when it's thrown around casually. When I express my love to someone, I want that person to know it's not a statement I simply toss around to anyone. It's the best I have to offer anyone and the best I can receive from anyone. The ultimate gift. So I want it to be pristine.

At the more mundane level of gift giving, I have my discomfort as well. When someone offers a gift, there is an expectation that the receiver will be excited, thankful, and affectionate. And, often, the gift giving itself is something obligatory prompted by a special occasion such as a birthday or graduation. In other words, the gift is as much social convention as an expression of the heart.

And, so, that scene has always been a weird mix for me. I want it to be simply authentic—a gift of the heart from someone I know truly cares at a time when I know their heartstrings have been plucked. But, too often it's not that straightforward.

When called upon to "act" like I love a present, or to "act" affectionate (hugs and kisses), or to act overwhelmed by the "love fest," the authenticity becomes murky. I don't like that. It's why I usually prefer that when I present a gift to someone they open it privately and not in my presence. But, I have grown to appreciate the value of social convention in its own right, and therefore the whole thing along with "forced" expectations is not as uncomfortable as it has been for me in the past.

Minutes

Left in that empty space
Of Time, to hear the whistle,
And hollow howl of nothingness.
Caught in the hailstorm of minutes.

Meanings

We're nervous in our black hole,
So we learn to make light
Of problems, pride, and busyness,
Veils of meaning in the night.

Nothing

Nothing hurts.
Hurt is nothing.
And nothing
Can help the hurt.

Nothing 2

Nothing is something,
And something hurts.
Oh, it's nothing,
Something just hurts.

Reflection on "Minutes" ...
"Nothing 2"

I t seems that human consciousness imbues us with the capacity to perceive a basic duality of our existence: namely, that our individual lives matter very little in the big scheme of things and that there is nothing more important than our individual lives. Philosophers have explored the anxiety we experience when we are most acutely aware of this duality. It is the "existential dilemma." And it is a challenge to comfortably hold two conflicting thoughts in mind at the same time. Yin and Yang. It is easier and more common to vacillate between one perspective and the other. "My life matters little and has no particular purpose" vs. "My life has purpose and meaning." Dark. Light. Awareness. Denial. These poems cover some of this landscape.

"Nothing is something." That was a revelation for me. It objectified something that otherwise was an ethereal menace. As "something," I could think of how to approach it, as opposed to the sense of helplessness I had confronting "nothing." The awareness of the giant existential abyss did not need to overwhelm me. Instead, it could just be another "something" to deal with.

The existential abyss is a concept that I have struggled with and continue to do so. When an empty space in time presents itself, I become uncomfortable. The emptiness can envelop me, and every click of the clock's second hand is like being pelted with a hailstone. There's

24

no escape since it's all around. Seconds, and minutes, and hours pelting me incessantly. One doesn't put an end to a hailstorm or escape it. All one can do is endure it. Wait it out. Take the whipping and hope it ends soon.

This can happen on weekends, weekday evenings, and even on vacation! I'll wake up in the morning with a whole day in front of me and nothing planned. What shall I do? I don't know. And then I feel the heated breath of "nothing" on my neck and begin to panic. My panic might lead me to busy myself. Puttering around. Making up stuff to do. Working.

If I am brave, I grab it (i.e., nothingness) by the scruff of its neck and begin wrestling with it. I do this by simply sitting still and calming myself down. It's my version of Muhammad Ali's "rope-a-dope." I tell myself to enjoy the moment, while the existential angst is trying to pin me to the mat.

Other times I just go into denial—"Oh, it's nothing" I tell myself, as I slough it off, allowing the irony to escape me. I try to dismiss it by trivializing it all. But then I'm left with a subterranean discomfort that is detached from its source. Something is bothering me, but I've disconnected it from its source—the existential abyss. Too often we deny the seriousness of our lack of control, of our dispensability, of the issues or dangers we face. That's how we manage to live our lives without being paralyzed by fear and anxiety.

Other times we actually exaggerate or make up "dangers" and problems as opposed to denying them so that we can derive meaning from a "righteous" fight. I saw so many people in my psychotherapy practice who derived their meaning from fighting, as it imbued them with a sense of self-righteous indignation. In order to let go of this contrarian approach to their life, our work required us to articulate a more constructive pursuit of meaning. Their psychological work was to move from finding meaning in "what I'm against" to "what I am for."

And, when I worked with people suffering with chronic pain, there was a small subset that were deriving their meaning from their pain. Prior to the slip and fall that initiated the pain, their lives seemed rather vapid. They found meaning in their suffering, in their ongoing pursuit of a solution, and in more time with, and attention from, family. The goal of pain *relief* was a psychological *threat* at a subconscious level. My work with them was less on pain relief strategies and more on finding meaningful activities to pursue despite their pain. When this strategy worked, their suffering diminished.

I continue my personal struggle by stalking meaningful activity and trying to appreciate the meaning in no-meaning. And, as I have contemplated retirement and have reduced my work commitments, I am all too aware of "the beast" of nothingness lurking!

Mindclearing

Trying to get these thoughts to leave,
They twist such a ratty, knotty weave,
When liquefied by sleep they'll spill,
Through the rain gutters of my mind.

REFLECTION ON "MINDCLEARING"

I tend to be obsessive, especially in regard to tasks. Things that I am working on run around and around in my head. My mind is scanning the task for errors, for stones left unturned, and for opportunities for improvement. It's like my mind is a proud problem-solver who attacks problems with a vengeance until they're resolved. I'm the law chasing the Fugitive—I will not rest until I've got my man. At times I love the feeling of being thoroughly consumed with something of interest.

At other times it's a monkey on my back that I want to shake loose. When I have numbers of projects or concerns happening concurrently, it feels like my mind goes into a state of tachycardia. At the right rate and rhythm, a heart pumps efficiently, but if it goes into hyperdrive (tachycardia), it loses almost all functionality. My mind goes into these states. A zillion things bouncing around to the point where I can't think my way out of a paper bag.

When my mind gets to spinning, it's time for a break. If I get away on vacation, after a few days I can usually let go of a lot of this. Then, when I return to normal life, things reenter my mind but not in their hyperenergetic form. Thoughts begin moving through my mind in a way that I can grab them and work with them.

This poem describes how sleep can also serve as this release valve—as a time to purge and then reconstruct.

Adequate sleep is so important and is something I could always depend on. Unfortunately, as I've grown older my sleep has become more disturbed and does not serve me as well as it did when I was younger.

Parenthetically, what I find interesting about myself in regard to being obsessive is that I am not very compulsive. I don't act on all my obsessions. This has its pluses and minuses. On the negative side, the lack of precisely organized and systematic action can delay me in getting things done. However, on the other hand, it keeps me from expending energy unnecessarily. Some ideas are better left to percolate before acting upon them.

Also, compulsiveness can tend to become an end instead of a means to an end. There are people who spend a good deal of energy organizing, planning, and developing procedural protocols for getting a task done. Form comes to take precedence over function. They take satisfaction that their daily planner is filled in properly, that organizational charts have been drawn, that strategic plans and visions and missions have been spelled out. Meanwhile, the task for which they are so meticulously planning has been delayed. Sometimes there's a quicker and more direct route to a final product. My lack of compulsiveness sometimes allows me to find these routes.

When all is said and done, there's nothing like a good night's sleep.

Sunset

Desperately pecking silent at sunset,
The earth, the bird needs food.
Then back to his nest for his restless rest,
We share a common mood.

REFLECTION ON "SUNSET"

I counseled a young man in his mid to late 20s who didn't know what to do with his life. He came from an upper-middle-class family and a culture in which kids went to college, chose a career, and then launched into that career by the age of 23. By the time they were 30 years old, they were "on track." They had boarded the train bound for success.

This young man couldn't seem to think of any direction worth committing himself to. He thought about it a lot—to the point of obsession. He felt the imminence of reaching 30 years old—sunset—and felt increasingly desperate about not having a direction. A vicious cycle established itself in which his anxiety interfered with his thinking, which in turn kept him stuck. And, because "time was running out," he felt his choice needed to be *just right*. In his mind he couldn't afford the luxury anymore of experimenting with different possibilities. Furthermore, since he was choosing *a career*, in his mind this was going to be his life's work—what he would be doing with the majority of his life for the next 40 years. If he made a mistake, he thought, he'd be doomed to a life that Thoreau referred to as one of "quiet desperation." So, he was "desperately pecking," trying to find some direction. He could not rest until he had this settled.

As with so many clients, my job was to help him calm down and work his way through his problem. I helped him understand that he was paralyzed. He was thinking but not doing. He wasn't actually trying different things, taking jobs, talking to people. He was all in his head. I let him know that his confusion belied some positive qualities—he was authentic, he was responsible, and he was thoughtful. He didn't want his life to be a fraud or to be wasted. It was precious, and he wanted to live it right.

I knew, though, as long as he was obsessed and panicked that his true interests could not emerge. They were buried. So, I helped him observe the reality that people take a variety of paths in life. That, although it seemed like everyone was on the same path, they really weren't. People discover their interests at all points in their life, and some never do. I let him know that some of the people who seemed to be on their way would wake up in their 40s to discover that they hadn't taken their early choices seriously enough and that they had spent the last 20 years doing something they didn't really like or value very much. I tried in these and other ways to create some breathing room—to allow him to enter a state of playfulness and exploration. It was difficult.

Finally, a private school asked him if he would fill in temporarily as a soccer coach. At first, he wasn't going to do it because he didn't think this was his ultimate calling and that it would therefore distract him from his search. But, as he realized it was temporary and that he needed to be *doing* in addition to *thinking*, he took the job. He loved working with the students and decided that he wanted to be a teacher. After resolving that he wouldn't become wealthy and that wealth wasn't a necessary measure of success, he moved forward. The weight of the world lifted from his shoulders! He smiled freely and began a relationship with a woman. He seemed reborn.

I personally experienced this sense of being desperately lost when I was in my early 20s. Luckily it only lasted a year or so. But what a miserable year it was. I felt like a racehorse stuck in a starting gate that wouldn't open. I wanted to run my race. My "muscles" were twitching to do it. But I had no direction. I didn't know what race to run. My breakthrough was a social psychology class I took in my senior year in college. It grabbed me. It became clear to me that psychology offered the opportunity of ongoing discovery and intellectual stimulation, as well as a variety of job possibilities in which I could make a contribution to others. I decided then to become a psychologist, and the weight of the world lifted.

And here I am now, so many years later, still fascinated with understanding human beings and eagerly working on a number of projects that I never could have guessed about back then. I have great sympathy for the pain of being lost and feel blessed that I found a way.

Maturity

My crystal prism eyes
Refract and separate
A simple ray of light,
I've learned to complicate.

REFLECTION ON "MATURITY"

Complexity crept up on me in my life. In my teens and young adulthood I more commonly experienced times of wonder and oneness with nature than when I moved into my thirties. There was something simple and clear when I was young. Ideals were clear and present—a simple ray of light. As I grew and my life became more complex with responsibilities, things became less clear and less simple. Those times of total rapture became less frequent. Ideals came with qualifiers. The clean beam of light became many beams bouncing in different directions—refracting and diffusing. One can meditate on a single beam of light. But bouncing and refracting light offers no focal point.

And so, I find that my mind, my attention, my consciousness bounce around now more than when I was young. Whereas it was once focused and clear, it has broken into many parts. I miss the simplicity. On the flip side, Life is richer for me than when I was younger. It can be luscious. But, more often than not, Life feels fragmented. Must be what Thoreau was thinking when he wrote, "Our life is frittered away by detail ... simplify, simplify."

Disillusioned

I pictured it in a rosy way,
Happening just as they all say,
I felt the wind kiss my head,
Then a swan in the sun farted.

REFLECTION ON "DISILLUSIONED"

Life is full of surprises, some of which just make you laugh. We get surprised because we develop expectations. Our capacity to project into the future and predict what will happen can be a great asset. In that way we can be prepared for what's next as opposed to being blindsided unprepared. Yet, like all great assets, this capacity to form expectations can be the bane of our existence, creating disappointment and hurt and the cascade of destructive behavioral expressions that emerge from those negative feelings.

We develop expectations of all sorts. A sunset is supposed to be beautiful. A wedding is supposed to be joyous. Family is supposed to be full of love. Hard work is supposed to be rewarded. Consideration is supposed to be returned. And it goes on and on and on.

Well, as I was walking through an aviary one beautiful spring day, I felt like I had entered a Norman Rockwell painting. Everything was as it should have been. The temperature was perfect, my mood was peaceful, and I felt great in body and spirit. It was romantic. I paused by the lake to watch the swans and the geese. The sun was sparkling on the water. The geese were dipping their heads in the water and then sending droplets of water spraying into the air as they shook their heads vigorously to shed the excess water they had taken on.

And then I caught sight of this absolutely stunning white swan—regal among its peers. It glided gracefully to the edge of the water, climbed out, and then, as best as I could guess, passed gas. I was stunned. My mind did a double take. Did I really just hear what I thought I had heard coming from where I thought I heard it come from? Do swans fart? I don't know why they wouldn't. But, I definitely know they *shouldn't*. Parents shouldn't have sex and mothers shouldn't belch.

It reminds me of a friend's daughter who grew up doing everything she was supposed to do. She worked hard—got straight A's, played sports, got involved in extra-curricular school activities, babysat, wore her seat belt, ate healthy foods—the whole nine yards. Then it came time to apply to college. She and her friends applied to some of the most competitive schools in the country. Her friends received acceptance letters—she didn't. She was devastated. She had trusted that the adults around her had taught her accurately the rules of this Game of Life. She had followed all the rules. She had done everything right. And then "the swan farted."

With some counseling and some time at the state school she had decided to attend, she grew up fast. She learned—not in an intellectual way, but in a cellular way—that life can be unfair. She learned that many people prefer to believe in myths of love and fairness to keep them from falling into despair and anxiety. And she discovered how free she could feel without the burden of all of the "shoulds." She rounded out her life and found this provided a fuller sense of satisfaction than achievement alone. The swan farted and set her free.

The work of the renowned psychologist Albert El-lis helped me and so many others recognize how our assumptions and expectations can create all sorts of problems for us when they are inaccurate. In his provocateur style he would say things like, "Don't sit on your ASSumptions," "Don't SHould on yourself," and "Don't MUSTerbate." I was surprised to discover how often words like "must," "should," and "have to" were in my thoughts and speech. Mostly they were exaggerations. I don't "have to" go to work today. I "could" stay home. Instead, all things considered, I "choose" to go to work today. I have no reason to believe that I "should" get my deserved rewards from hard work and good intentions, as fairness is not a core organizing principle of Life. Nowhere is it written that I should be treated nice if I treat others nice. It's just amazing how many trip hazards get removed from the path of Life when you clear out inaccurate expectations.

Swans fart. I'll be damned! A visual image reminding me to check my assumptions and expectations.

Cokeahol

Jagged, ragged, granite edge,
Torqueing in my head.
Spirits smooth a comfort salve,
And the world is mine to have.

REFLECTION ON "COKEAHOL"

M any years ago I facilitated a discussion panel of teen-agers during a public forum on teen use of drugs and alcohol. It was in a well-to-do suburb. The parents and other adults were concerned about the prevalence of substance use. They ostensibly wanted to hear from "the horse's mouth" why this was so rampant. Of course, as it turned out, they didn't really want to listen as much as they wanted to have a chance to lecture the kids about the wrongness of using drugs and alcohol. Unfortunately, from my point of view, the youths began to parrot what they thought they were supposed to say. So the forum quickly became a series of little monologues about how people use drugs because they're bored or because they're trying to escape a negative reality. While this can certainly be true, it explains only a little about teen drug use.

Then, a brave young man raised his hand. He was fed up with all the folderol and threw out a zinger. "Kids get high because it's fun and it feels good!" BAM! Speak truth to power, baby. I tried to keep this line of discussion alive, but it died quickly. It was so real, but I could tell the question running through people's minds was "What do we do with that? We know it's true, and we can't argue against fun and pleasure." So they dropped it.

People are drawn to altered states. Altered states are interesting. Little kids like to be held upside down and swung around, adults like amusement rides and drinking, and we all watch movies and read books which transport us from our realities somewhere else. And, let's not forget, teens like to flirt with breaking adult rules; and they like to play with their emerging adultness by playing with adult toys like cars, cigarettes, and alcohol. They always have and probably always will.

Using drugs and alcohol has different meanings for different people at different times. For some it's escape, for others it's a method of self-medicating, for others it's recreation, and for others it can be an aid in a spiritual search. Substances themselves are not bad any more than an automobile is bad because of its powerful potential to hurt and kill. Automobiles kill mainly when drivers exercise poor judgment. In turn, how people choose to use chemical substances can be good choices or bad choices. Admittedly this analogy falls short in that alcohol and many drugs can be more addictive than driving cars.

Some people are prone to poor judgment, and the implications of their poor judgments are related to the tools they play with, whether those be drugs, guns, sex, or motor vehicles. What if the focus in our society was on making good personal choices rather than prescribing and proscribing choices broadly? What might this look like? I think it would entail encouraging self-knowledge and appreciation of individual diversity. We would study what we know about our own species as much or more than studying other species. We'd learn about relationships, communication, conflict resolution, goal setting, cognitive errors we are vulnerable to, self-regulation, etc. We would come to know ourselves better and thereby develop a better internal compass for navigating life and for appreciating others.

Speck

Just a speck, that's all I am,
Dancing around my speck-land,
Casting big shadows for all to see,
Just a speck ... that's all I am.

Existence

I have not spoken for years,
Eons have invaded my blood.
In awe and poignant solitude,
I am stunned by my existence.

REFLECTION ON "SPECK" ... "EXISTENCE"

Many times in my life, and less often as I get older, I experience moments when I sense myself in unison with Time and the entire Cosmos. At once I am as tiny as tiny can get, yet I am the essential battery powering a flashlight. Individual life has no importance in the scheme of things, yet without individual life, there would be no life. When I am at the exact intersection of this paradox I feel peaceful and blessed. My voice seems to be silenced by the greatness and wonder of Life. My words and actions are so small as to render me effectively mute and motionless. I stand alone, surrounded by an immensity that has its own momentum and direction. What I say or do matters little ... in the Big Scheme.

At times my smallness makes me uncomfortable, almost panicky. If nothing I say or do matters, it is like I have died, or am dying. Panic sets in. I rush to action. I retreat to busyness. I puff my chest out with self-importance. Ughhh. I hate being like that.

The flip side of that coin is feeling a calm that I think is associated with a sense of relief from personal responsibilities. If my life is so little and there is a bigger play in motion, then I need not worry so much about what I do. I can let go ... can give it over to a bigger process. I can't mess things up very much. Even if I'm lax, it doesn't really matter. And I can't make much of a positive impact either. It feels like a freeing from responsibility. I am part of something miraculous and can play my part amongst the Many.

Mainly I am in neither of the above states—neither panicked nor calmly relieved. Instead I am just living my life without the BIG perspective in mind. Over the years I have become increasingly comfortable with this great duality. What I do with my life doesn't matter at all, and at the same time it's all that matters. For it is all that I have.

Life Sounds

Crickets and birds,
Singing in thirds,
Every living thing,
Trying to be heard.

Hurt

I shared with you some poetry,
A part of me, my core,
My heart tore when you said, "How nice,"
But never asked for more.

Safety Knot

No one seems to understand,
So I stay to myself a lot.
And the less I show, the less they know,
Bound by my safety knot.

Safe

No one knows me.
I won't let them know.
To know me
Is to know you can't know.

Silent

I will not speak,
You shall not know,
I'm just not ready,
For yet another blow.

Trust

I'm no good at trusting,
Been burned too bad before,
So I see shadows lurking,
Near every open door.

REFLECTION ON "LIFE SOUNDS" ... "TRUST"

We all long to be understood and accepted. It hurts when we are misunderstood, ignored, or rejected. The hurt is deep since the need is deep. This is a series of poems about these hurts experienced by me, people I have known, and psychotherapy clients of mine, and some adaptations that create dysfunction. Repeated hurts condition us to respond in any of the following ways.

One response is to live LOUDER trying to seek attention and approval. Showing off. Bragging. Narcissistic self-centeredness. Sometimes this leads to our need for recognition being met, and this rewarded "look at me!" behavior becomes a personality style—a habitual way of being in the world. Other times, like a cracked vessel being filled with water, the need for recognition never seems fulfilled and the behavior persists on the backdrop of angst. It is unrewarding to be with people like this because it is all about them—they suck all the air out of the room—there's no place for others to be recognized. And the admiration they obtain for their achievements does not satisfy their need to be understood and accepted for who they are inside. Only when human-*being* and human-*doing* are overlapping does deep fulfillment occur.

And, if approval is not in the cards for us, then attention itself—even if it's negative—will suffice. I saw the latter often when I worked as a psychologist in the juvenile justice system and when I was a child care worker with children removed from their families by the state. These kids would act out in ways they knew would get them into trouble. They weren't even trying hard to escape detection. In a way, it was befuddling. But I came to appreciate how the alternative of being ignored was a worse fate. The challenge working with these kids was to help them come to experience reasons why they might hold out hope of being able to obtain *positive* attention.

Another response to repeated existential hurt is to learn how to be in the world without revealing too much of the "real" you. You learn to try to match your self-presentation with what you think and hope people want of you. In that way you might attain a modicum of acceptance while at the same time protecting yourself from rejection/disapproval of who you really are. This kind of acceptance, though, is somewhat hollow. It is not fulfilling. The protectiveness is comforting, but isolating and lonely.

"Safety Knot" describes this dilemma. The less time they spend "out of their shell," the less opportunity there is for them to get what they really want—recognition and acceptance for who they really are. They become doomed. They set the course for their destiny and lock it in. And, as described in the poem "Trust," some people err in the direction of suspecting rejection even when it is not there. These are folks who take offense if you simply look at them the "wrong" way.

"Silent" is about a young woman whom I worked with in a psychiatric hospital. She was the only child of two psychologists. Far from her being ignored, they pushed her to express her *every* thought and feeling. They were well intentioned. They were overly attentive, and it felt invasive to their daughter. She felt overexposed. In this circumstance, she became a "turtle." She became locked up inside of herself.

On top of this reticence was an overlay of resistance—a passive-aggressiveness. Her agenda was not only to protect herself, but also to foil attempts by others (symbolically her "parents") to "lure" her out of her shell. She was angry for being put in that position and was lashing back with her guarded style. She was locked up tighter than anyone I ever met. She was tough, but so sad and mad. It was only in a state of panic about this self-imprisonment that she reached out with a suicide attempt. But in the hospital she couldn't sustain her courage to BE. She began to open up long enough for her panic to subside and then clamped shut. I think she reflexively closed up as therapists pushed and probed like her parents had done so often. Her habits took over, and as far as I know, no one ever wedged themselves far enough in to keep the door open. She did not get what she needed.

We can all do better in acknowledging and supporting each other if we shift our intention from getting to giving and trust the human inclination toward reciprocity. Sometimes the best way to be loved is to give love.

Attributions

I cried, so I must be weak.
And my weakness makes me meek.
Meek and weak I slink around,
Crying, to prove my thinking is sound.

REFLECTION ON "ATTRIBUTIONS"

The brain is tasked with a challenge to take in information, organize it, and remain flexible to expand its organizational structure as new information comes in that doesn't fit well into the structures it has already formed. In the research field of information processing this process consists of "assimilation" and "accommodation."

Assimilation is the part of the process of fitting incoming information into existing conceptual categories. For example, as we experience our family pets, and the pets of friends, we may form the construct that all animals with certain characteristics that qualify them as dogs or cats may become known as "friendly pets." Then we encounter an unfriendly dog walking with their owner. That creates an uncomfortable psychological state called "cognitive dissonance"—when a new experience is not consistent with what we expect based on how we already understand things. If we *assimilate* that experience, we may think that this is another friendly pet dog that *for some reason* is acting unfriendly. In doing this we are pushing a not-quite-circular object into a round hole, so to speak. To stretch the example further, if a first encounter with a snake was in the wild and we assimilated that into our "friendly pet" construct, it would be more like jamming a square peg into a round hole. We would fail to develop the construct of "wild animals" and the realization that not all animals are "friendly pets." Research in the area of *selective inattention* indicates that we also can tend to not even pay attention to things that we can't assimilate easily. We actually don't hear and see certain things! As Simon and Garfunkel so aptly put in their song "The Boxer," "Still a man hears what he wants to hear and disregards the rest." While overassimilating things into our existing mental constructs may take less energy and create less anxiety, it runs the risk of disconnecting us from fully understanding things as they really are. We can distort reality as we assimilate information.

Alternatively, we might *accommodate* that experience of the growling and attacking dog by forming a new construct that there are also "unfriendly pets." In this way, our understanding of our world becomes increasingly complex. Overaccommodation ends up also creating anxiety related to ever-increasing complexity and energy expenditure trying to make sense of things.

Without these processes of assimilation and accommodation working in a balanced fashion, our understanding of our life experiences would become either too overwhelmingly complex and chaotic or so rigidly narrow as to oversimplify and prevent effective learning. Our ongoing accumulation of knowledge, and ultimately wisdom, requires that we flexibly and fluidly cycle through accommodating and assimilating information in an artful way. And, I think we cannot do that well without help from others, especially when we lose flexibility by dampening our willingness to form new ideas.

In my psychotherapy office I would repeatedly see unbalanced information processing leading to dysfunctional living. For example, after a number of negative experiences with men, a young child might develop the construct that "men are mean." Without adequate accommodating, experiences with men who were *not* mean became lumped into the same idea that "all men are mean." As a woman, this would then lead to relationship problems with men, either in the form of avoiding intimate relationships with men or of overinterpreting men's behaviors as mean. Successful therapy in cases like this resulted from helping the client *accommodate* her experiences with nice men by expanding her understanding to "some men are mean/untrustworthy, and some are friendly/trustworthy." As a psychotherapist I saw many variations on the above theme, and the guiding insight I was always shooting to impart is captured in the phrase "That was then, this is now." In other words, in your past maybe it seemed like all men were mean, but this is now, and you can observe directly that some men are not mean and dispute the erroneous idea you had formed earlier in life.

Another manifestation of this information processing balancing act going awry forms the backdrop of the poem "Attributions."

I was working with a young woman whose organizing concept about herself was "I am weak." This was the legacy of her parents, who told her in too many ways while she was young that she was weak, and that weak was bad. It started with crying. Crying is a fundamental and universal human behavior. As an infant it is a primary way to communicate displeasure. Most adults try to get kids to stop crying—either to alleviate distress or, too often, because it can just be so irritating to the adult. As we grow past infancy into childhood, many people are told that crying is a sign of weakness and something to be suppressed. To wit, the parent I recently observed scolding his ten-year-old boy who was crying after falling and scraping his knee, "Don't be a baby!" This young woman I was working with had received heaping doses of negative judgment about her crying from an early age.

Her mind, therefore, organized the concept of "I am a weak person." She would ignore signs of strength—for example, the courage it took to enter therapy, or her work ethic—and instead would attend to everything that spelled w-e-a-k. Her mind was seeking consistency. She was stuck in a vicious cycle—she *thought* of herself as weak, therefore *acted* weak, which in turn strengthened her self-concept of *being* weak. In psychology this is referred to as a *negative self-fulfilling prophecy*. The course of therapy involved shifting to a *positive self-fulfilling prophecy*—that is, a self-concept of strength—of activating her innate process of accommodation.

I did this by pointing out strength when I observed it in her stories. For example, as she complained about always being mistreated by boyfriends, I could point out her "perseverance," her "optimism and persistent hopefulness," her "dedication" and "loyalty." I would ask her to do things or talk about things that I knew were difficult for her, and then point out the strengths I saw. Over time, the seed of this concept grew, and lo and behold, she became less meek and less prone to crying, and began building a life on the self-concepts of being perseverant, loyal, optimistic, brave, etc.

Personally, I was fortunate to have a mother who set in motion for me a self-concept of being "trustworthy." She did not police me closely, instead choosing to say in actions and words, "I trust you because you are worthy of my trust." I can remember conforming my behavior to fit this construct because I didn't want to experience the guilt of disappointing her, and because it is how I came to think of myself. The result is the self-fulfilling prophecy that has guided my behavior more than less—to be a responsible and trustworthy person. I thank her for her wisdom.

Strength

Oak branch broke
From piled-on snow,
Weak willow bowed,
To greet the spring doe.

REFLECTION ON "STRENGTH"

I t was not until I was a young adult that I realized why
trees lose their leaves in the fall. An early October
snowfall one year left tree limbs littered throughout
the city. The leaves were little platforms on which the
snow piled until the weight was so great that the limb
snapped. The bigger and older the tree, the greater
the damage. The young and weak trees bent instead
of breaking. When the snow melted, the younger trees
stretched their aching backs gingerly until they stood,
once again, upright. They survived to see the spring.
The big strong trees broke.

This was such a graphic demonstration of one of Life's
paradoxes—that in weakness lies strength. In the
weakness of emotional sensitivity lies the strength of
self-awareness and empathy. In the weakness of ambiv-
alence comes the time for measured consideration. In
the weakness of apology lies the strength of reconcilia-
tion. This snowstorm gave me an *Aha!* on the prophecy
"the meek shall inherit the earth."

I have seen so many people in therapy who benefited
from absorbing this lesson personally. Men, who think
that strength is defined by emotional stoicism, strong
and unbending opinions, willpower, and … simply
power in and of itself. Women, who have been told over
and over again that they are "too sensitive," meaning
that they misconstrue things and overreact emotionally. Men would have them believe they are "crazy" and

emotionally weak. As a therapist, my goal was to help these people come to embrace their "weaknesses" and to understand them as strengths.

I used to be one of those men. I know stubbornness well and how to avoid vulnerability. And I know that these stances make me feel strong on one hand and impotent on the other. There's a sense of being protected but being ineffective. Like a turtle, I can withdraw into my shell, but then I just sit still. Nothing moves forward or gets accomplished. I feel small but safe.

My wife has been relentless in her efforts to make me talk when I want to retreat. I eventually discovered that opening up made me more vulnerable but more effective. I felt less safe but much "bigger"—more in control. I could do *my* part in getting arguments resolved as opposed to having them linger and repeat themselves. When I stopped trying to control everything, lo and behold, I had more control! Putting up fewer and less imposing barricades allowed love to flow between us. And so I learned that being "weak"—that is, sensitive, open-minded, and flexible—was actually a strength.

And I was fortunate to observe firsthand the positive dimensions of my wife's emotional sensitivity. She is more empathically understanding. She creates closer friendships. She more readily perceives hidden agendas and undermining processes when people are working together. This allows her to "cut to the quick" of things. And, she gets excited at levels I don't achieve!

It was always so gratifying as a therapist to help a woman, or especially a couple, discover the wonder and strength in a woman's emotionality. The women's heads would tilt up, their eyes open wider, and their posture straighten as their spouse came to understand her emotionality differently. The women quickly abandoned "victimhood" and embraced their personal agency. "Oversensitivity" became "exquisite sensitivity." They possessed strengths that they hadn't understood as such. With new understanding they came alive! And couples achieved truer intimacy.

The Tear

It grew so heavy and sprang from the corner,

Dropping thru the creases on the face of
the mourner,

Pausing at the lips which will smile
again tomorrow,

Then drawn in by the tongue tip for the tasting of
the sorrow.

REFLECTION ON "THE TEAR"

E motions run a course. They have that characteristic in common with fluids. This is one of the most important lessons I've learned in life, for it is the source of hope during hard times. Many people seek a permanent state of happiness, or dread getting stuck in a permanent state of despair. The reality is, though, that Nature has a rhythm of ebbs and flows. Everything alive vibrates. From subatomic particles to the vicissitudes of our individual lives, Life unfolds in the shape of a sine curve. And so it is with emotions. They ebb and flow. Our task in coping with emotions is to allow them to run their course—to not get in their way—to avoid damming them. Like the tear in this poem, an emotion will flow a natural course. In accepting the emotion—*drawn in by the tongue tip*—we allow it to run its course, which means that we allow it to resolve—to leave.

It is when we try to overmanage our emotions that we get in trouble. I think of emotions like the water in a river. They can run calm and they can run rough and intense. When they are intense and the current is strong, one is advised to "go with the flow" rather than fight it. Like a person in a canoe, rough waters call for you to stay alert and centered and ride it out. It is when one tries to control the situation by turning toward shore that the current asserts its way and capsizes the canoe.

Unfortunately, we are raised in a culture in which we are supposed to control things, and in which negative emotional states must not be tolerated. So, in response to being sad, or angry, or depressed, many people try to rid themselves of the emotion as quickly as possible. They deny, rationalize, pretend, ignore, distract themselves, etc. But, without the acceptance, the emotion swirls around in an eddy, trying to release itself but remaining stuck inside. It is one of the basic paradoxes in life. To control an emotion is to lose control of it, and to let go is to gain some control.

As a therapist I used to demonstrate this to people by asking them to tell me how they were feeling in the moment. They might say "depressed" or "anxious." Then I would ask them to hold that emotion perfectly still ... to not let it increase or decrease in intensity. Nine times out of ten they would smile as they felt the emotion dissipate. These were not miraculous cures. They were demonstrations. People left that experience not so much with great relief but with some hope. "If I stop trying so hard to fight it, it may leave sooner than later." I have come to trust this law of Nature and hope that this trust will endure and provide me, too, with some hope and reassurance when I am struggling.

The Motions

She motions through work quite well,

Like everyone else, but she knows,

That when the bus lets her off at her lonely loft,

In a sleeping bag, on the floor, she'll go.

REFLECTION ON "THE MOTIONS"

I saw the woman who is the subject of this poem in therapy. She was about 35 and was depressed. She was an office manager at a midsize manufacturing company. She dressed in business attire, wore makeup, and styled her hair. She was a reliable employee and did a good job. She was friendly and smiled readily.

But she did not socialize outside of work. Not just in regard to her co-workers. At all! As we talked, I was first surprised to learn she rode the bus each day. Nothing especially unusual in and of itself. Just unexpected given her apparent station in life. I would have expected that she owned a modest car and drove to work. She did not own a car. Then she described her apartment. It was sparse to the point of being bare. It struck me strongly when she told me she had no bed. She slept in a sleeping bag on a hardwood floor!

I knew she wasn't financially impoverished. But her impoverished sense of self was stunning. She did not think she deserved such things as couches, chairs, and a bed. It didn't take much time to discover the roots of this in the scorched internal landscape that was her childhood. She was largely ignored and often disrespected. No one threw her birthday parties. She did not receive gifts at Christmas. There were no outings to fairs or amusement parks. She basically learned that she was undeserving and unimportant. As with so many clients, recognizing a cause in the past freed her to consider that maybe things didn't need to stay that way in the present. As I've stated so many times in therapy, "That was then. This is now." She recognized she had a lot more to say about her life as an adult than she did as a dependent child.

And so, with much trepidation and reassurance she began to venture out socially. Small things at first—hanging out a little longer at the office watercooler. Then having lunch with some women co-workers. Then she began to develop some women friends. And then a date with a man! She broke free. I knew things had changed dramatically when she bought a car. I imagine her having a house now filled to the brim with all sorts of things.

To some degree, life for each of us can be like a masquerade ball. We present ourselves "appropriately" to fit in. We let people know certain parts of ourselves and protect or hide other parts. If we are lucky, we find at least one person with whom we feel safe enough to reveal parts of ourselves otherwise hidden from the public.

When it comes to people, we need to read the book beyond its cover—beyond the masks we don for the public.

Scary Lady

The lady with the creases, sunken eyes, and the dimple,

Sorrow etched deep, nothing very simple,

People stay away so she's lonely for a friend,

But her face frightens them as they're trying to pretend.

REFLECTION ON "SCARY LADY"

The emotional pains in life can be so intense. We try to avoid pain, but some of us end up with a load of it that keeps accumulating over time. Bad luck and poor decisions seem to be the culprits. And then there's the issue of suffering from persistent pain. Two people can experience equal pain, and one might suffer worse than the other. The Greek philosopher Epictetus said something to the effect of "Man is not bothered by things as much as what he thinks of things." By virtue of constitution and learning, some people are ill-equipped to manage their emotional pain. They make one bad decision that leads to a string of negative consequences reaching far and wide into their lives. They're dealt bad hands and have never learned how to play their cards. Over time, their faces seem to bear scars from emotional injury.

It has been interesting observing how people deal with the fact that to live and be in relationships is to be vulnerable to painful experiences. On one hand, we have a host of avoidance strategies—distractions, self-medicating with alcohol/drugs, denying reality via distorting perceptions to see only what we want to see, and repressing and compartmentalizing things that bring pain when they enter our consciousness. On the other hand, we seem to spend a lot of time and money trying to inoculate ourselves against life's painful exigencies as we reward media for providing us with an unending stream of movies, books, and news about humans acting badly and life tragedies. So, while we try to avoid and minimize experiencing emotional pain, we prepare ourselves by indirectly experiencing it.

When it comes to relationships, it is a rare person who leans into truth when doing so brings hurt. Instead, we tend to pretend to ourselves that our pain is not there and that it is not "out there" coming to get us, so to speak. We avoid people with pain plastered across their faces. We avoid people who are bold and indelicate truth speakers. As much as possible, we'd like to be in our safe bubble where everything is just fine.

Though a bit different, reflecting on this brings up my avoidance of visiting my father's grave. I was blessed that he lived to be 90 years old, but when he died, my heart was crushed. My north star disappeared from my night sky. It was a deep bruise as opposed to a surface cut. When we lowered him into the ground, and when I threw a shovel of dirt on his coffin and walked to the side, my legs went out and I was on my knees slamming the ground with my fists. I have never been back to visit. I'm afraid of the pain.

The Waver

He shuffles along down the main street,
On his daily medicinal stroll,
Mechanically waving to strangers in cars,
And then back to his nursing home hole.

REFLECTION ON "THE WAVER"

H umans are social animals. It is one of our basic characteristics. We are wired to find some attachment of acceptance with others; that is, to achieve a sense of belonging. And, in service of our survival instincts, we jostle around in many ways for status and access to valued resources by associating ourselves selectively with people who can make connections with others, open opportunities, help us if we become in need, and otherwise elevate our social status and sense of self-worth. Further, we are wired to find relationships in which we can give and receive love, relationships of intimacy. My mnemonic for this is "in/out, top/down, near/far," expressing these as the dimensions of relationships that matter to us. We can achieve a sense of belonging from acquaintance relationships, such as being a member of a faith community, a hobby group, and an ethnic/cultural group. We can achieve intimacy with romantic relationships and close friendships. And, our jockeying for status can occur across all relationships. Regarding the latter, we can fulfill this need to some degree by community-valued prowess and achievements, by proxies of the latter such as displays of wealth and recognition, and indirectly by relationships with people of power, means, and reputation. I have found that I can make sense of most of my observations of myself and others in relationship within this framework. In my role as a psychotherapist, I also found that this framework could be helpful to clients. Commonly I would find that clients were trying to achieve intimacy with acquaintances or casual friendships ... as country music performer Johnny Lee sang, "looking for love in all the wrong places." It could be helpful for them to align their expectations in a relationship based on whether it was an acquaintance, a nonintimate friendship (a person to do things with), or an intimate relationship. Bottom line is we need people—to be in relationship.

I used to have a daily travel route that had me driving by a nursing home at the same time each day. Except for inclement days, there was an old man in a wheelchair who had his assistant push him to the edge of the sidewalk facing the street. He would smile and wave wholeheartedly to every car that passed. I'd wave back and then always have a sick feeling in the pit of my stomach that would linger until interrupted. I imagined the loneliness and desperation that was the backdrop of his daily routine. No family. Caretaking without real connection inside. Eternities of minutes feeling detached from the world. It broke my heart.

John Prine, in my opinion one of the elite singer-songwriters of the twentieth century, captured this poignantly in his song "Hello in There." The chorus in that song is:

> *You know that old trees just grow stronger*
> *And old rivers grow wilder every day*
> *Old people just grow lonesome*
> *Waiting for someone to say, "Hello in there... hello."*

Validation

Knowing of mirages in this desert land,

Before I quench I touch with my hand,

Raised to doubt all that I perceive,

I cry just to know that I'm sad.

REFLECTION ON "VALIDATION"

We are endowed with sensory capacities to gather information and with a mind to make sense of our observations, resulting in perceptions. Our sensory capacities are limited, as became evident to me as a young boy observing my dog hearing things beyond my capacity. He heard certain wavelengths that I could not hear, letting me know at that early age that I was only able to sense a portion of reality, and therefore there were likely many things in reality beyond my abilities to sense and understand. And our minds have a variety of filters for processing the information we sense. These filters cause us to pay more or less attention to aspects of our experiences depending on our psychological needs, fears, and desires. Simon and Garfunkel wrote in "The Boxer," "A man hears what he wants to hear and disregards the rest." That has seemed to enter my mind so often across the years, especially as I have observed how split our country is politically. People are observing the same things but processing them to such different conclusions. Research in cognitive processing uncovered a phenomenon called "cognitive dissonance" which revealed discomfort, and therefore avoidance tendencies, when incoming information is incongruent with the way we have come to understand things. Hence, if we think that young African American men are prone to criminality, we will extract information from a situation that is consistent with that when we observe them—thus racial profiling. If we expect that someone is trying to "one-up" us, then we interpret their question as an aggressive move as opposed to an expression of curiosity. I often have a comportment that conveys to others that I am criticizing and trying to elevate myself above them, which has left me feeling misunderstood when I am coming from a place of curiosity, and that is met with defensiveness and upset.

Not only do we tend to see others according to our expectations about them, but we do the same with ourselves—acting in accordance with what we have come to expect of ourselves based on self-image and self-narratives. When I worked as a psychologist in a juvenile justice center, I observed this often whereby youth were acting in accordance with their self-image of "I'm a rule breaker," as an example. As a psychotherapist with adults, I often observed people acting in accordance with their conclusions about themselves, such as "I am weak," "I am stupid," or "I make bad decisions." That became a vicious cycle in which their ideas about themselves drove their behavior which, in turn, further cemented their ideas. Helping them unpack the stories they hold in mind about themselves and discover any errors therein could help them break free of negative behaviors.

Also, some people who have been so overwhelmed with negative emotions shut down their emotion system, dimming it as much as they can. Numbness is good when all you expect to feel is pain. It is one thing when a person feels in control of what they feel and don't feel, and quite another when they feel like their finger can no longer turn "the light" on and off as desired, and instead, the light is stuck in "off." Numbness then feels like death. I observed in those cases that, in an effort to feel *something*, people would act as if they were sad or angry.

My father expressed the flip side of that by acting as if he was happy when he wasn't. As a young man who experienced lots of physical suffering and a close brush with death, he found that if he acted as if everything was fine, he could keep the suffering from being a ball and chain that would sink him. There were so many times I knew he was feeling bad emotionally or physically and would ask him how he was feeling, and he would break out a big put-on smile and say in a strong voice, "Great." Many times, in the moment, that bothered me as it came off as inauthentic and did nothing to bring us closer. As I grew into adulthood and gained insight into why he did this, it morphed from being bothersome to stirring sadness and compassion … for his suffering and for the distance it created between us. But, there were other times that I saw his ability to execute "mind over matter" as amazing and even heroic. When my sister got married, he became ill with a virus that I had recently recovered from. So I knew how bad he felt. But, as a father, he was not going to rain on his daughter's parade. At the party he took the father-daughter dance with full zest, then discreetly left to vomit and regain his energy so he could head back out and be the life of the party. I recall it as a heroic act of love.

Pinball

Tomorrow has gone
The way of my past,
So like a pinball I must
Stay frenetic and fast.

REFLECTION ON "PINBALL"

The future is the realm of possibilities and choice, and, of course, uncertainty. Uncertainty often makes us uncomfortable, and so we avoid it as we can. I have encountered times in my life when I have felt like I was abdicating my responsibility of choice about where I was headed and hiding in the comfort of where the momentum of my life was taking me. Streams of life can have strong undercurrents. It's easier to go with the flow than change direction, not knowing exactly how that new direction will turn out. Besides experiencing it myself, I observed it with clients and with friends and family. In those capacities I've known spouses who remain in a marriage not due to satisfaction or love, but because the thought of making a change entails so much uncertainty and effort. I've known people who remain in jobs for the same reason as opposed to the meaning or fulfillment derived from the work. Henry David Thoreau famously said, "The mass of men lead lives of quiet desperation." It gives my soul indigestion to digest the truth in that observation. As any of us are satisficing, we run from the realization of doing so. Often, we do so by busying ourselves with activity that distracts us from recognizing our "desperation." Bouncing from this thing to the next, allowing outside forces to pull us forward as opposed to facing the tougher task of pushing ourselves forward with the internal forces of our interest, passions, and aspirations. I do try to pause myself and smell the roses.

Pleasing

Yes ma'am, no ma'am, if I could,
I'd do everything that I should,
Never think for-about myself.
Sucked dry deep inside.

REFLECTION ON "PLEASING"

From the moment of birth when we are handed over to the arms of an adult, our lives unfold with some degree of tension between becoming and being who we are and pleasing those around us. As social beings, other people matter ... A LOT. We come to discern whose approval matters the most to us and whose approval matters little. We all have a pleasing gene, metaphorically speaking.

Who we are is some combination of our genetic composition and environmental conditions. To the degree our environment enables the unfolding of genetic predispositions, we come to be comfortable in our own skin and possess self-acceptance and confidence. But, to the degree that the people that matter to us expect and require us to be different from how we are naturally inclined, we experience tension and pain that results, in different degrees, in self-loathing, shame, and insecurity. Our millions of social interactions fall along this continuum of supporting and nurturing who we are or requiring us to deform ourselves to get the goodies we need from others—acceptance, respect, love. Our experience of feeling pressure to conform and deform ourselves to others' expectations and desires falls along a continuum of a small painful injury to a traumatic assault. So many of us luckily avoid traumatic experiences, yet experience the accumulation of minor injuries. I refer to this as "the picador effect," referring to the horsemen (picadors) who jab small spears into a bull's shoulders prior to the bullfighter entering the ring. None of these injuries are serious, but they do serve to anger the bull and to cause it to drop its head with the weakening that occurs from the accumulation of the small assaults. So too, the many small injuries to our selves incurred by what we perceive to be the expectations of others accumulate and cause our posture to begin drooping, metaphorically speaking. Instead of approaching life in an erect stance with eyes forward, standing tall, we become bent over with our eyes on the ground ... insecure and lacking confidence. The more we feel insecure, the more important the approval from others becomes, and a vicious cycle is set in motion. A person can get so wrapped up in that cycle that they become separated from themselves, from their voice within, and preoccupied with pleasing others to such an extent as to become an empty shell of themselves. So sad.

Partying

Flying through with frozen ease,
Try to catch me if you please,
I'll just smile and be polite.
Escaping through the night.

REFLECTION ON "PARTYING"

I've always hated parties. For one, I feel awkward. I don't care much for chitchat or for the social positioning going on or the expectation of "having fun." I do like small gatherings where people connect with one another authentically and share in fun. But the larger gatherings where there is no intention to connect deeply, but instead to splash around on the surface making a lot of noise, just leave me empty.

I do recognize that lots of people have a more fluid personality than I do, more readily moving from the seriousness of life to frivolity, all the while retaining their authenticity. But I also know people can be acting as if they are having fun or running from seriousness to superficiality, and I feel it when I'm in it. It makes me uneasy. I hate interacting with someone and feeling that I never even met them, as there were so many layers of self-presentational impression management bullshit blocking the way to them. And I hate talking with someone who is looking over my shoulder and all around for what is happening and who else they might want to go over and talk with next. I accept that I can be boring to folks. I don't know gossip and don't track sports and entertainers or the weather. And, I think I determined early in my life that only a very small circle of people really matter to me, and so I don't have much motivation to mix it up with others. When I do have a motivation, such as if there's a gathering of people who matter to my interests in what I'm doing in life, I can be cordial and "work the room," but it takes a lot out of me. I'm drained and emotionally dulled afterwards.

One of the rewards of being a psychotherapist was that I could spend my days connecting meaningfully with people. That could be energizing. But there were also many times when I worked hard and failed at making a connection. It was like my client was a buoy floating on the surface of the water, and I was trying to drag them underwater to their internal depths. Resistance all the way. It must have felt the same to them. If I managed to outmuscle them psychologically, the minute I let go they'd pop back to the surface. There were so many people with whom I was unsuccessful in trying to help. That being said, I always remind myself of a fascinating book I read by Irvin Yalom and his psychotherapy client called *Every Day Gets a Little Closer* in which they separately chronicled their therapy encounters, revealing that when one of them thought their sessions were unproductive, the other sometimes thought just the opposite. So, you never really know the impact you have on other people. Personal growth is a process of many experiences coming together over time and an often unexpected clicking together to create meaning at particular moments.

Dog in Grass

He nuzzles his nose in the past,
Seeking scents that are stored in his bones,
The baking sun and cushion of grass,
Take him back where his spirit roams.

REFLECTION ON "DOG IN GRASS"

The brilliant psychoanalyst Carl Jung explored with great scholarliness the idea that human beings carry with them knowledge and intelligence that derive not only from their individual genetics and experiences, but also from the previous experiences of their ancestors and species over the course of human evolution. We are moved by forces that are present, but there are also forces which guide our lives that are rooted deeply in the past. Though our lives may seem quite disconnected from the lives of our predecessors, they are connected in some ways that cannot be dissected and discerned. Am I the way I am in part because my parents are who they are? Yes. And are my parents the way they are in part due to their parents? Yes. And were my grandparents the way they were in part due to the influence of teachers, friends, neighbors, etc.? Yes. And so, there is this interconnectedness between us all that links us to our past—a "collective unconscious."

I have emphasized this sense of heritage with my children. I have told them to think about their first and last names as they guide themselves through their lives. Their first name represents their individuality. And their last name represents their family and ethnic lineage. I tell them that if they consider their actions from both of these vantage points, they will probably make pretty good decisions over time.

Their lives are ultimately theirs to shape. They must honor their first name, their individuality. That's why it comes first. Make your life an expression of your individuality ... who you are. But, temper your choices with consideration of your heritage. "Your actions not only reflect on you as an individual but are your contributions to a long story—a story of your lineage. You have your chance to write chapters in a long book, and you need to think about what you want your passages to say." That's the message. I've taken criticism for conveying this message because some others perceive it as laying a "guilt trip" on my kids to get them to conform. That's not it at all. It's about understanding your life as something bigger than just yourself—understanding heritage. In any case, like so many lessons taught in parenting, I'm not so sure if this one ever registered.

So, when my young son stole a bike, I had the following conversation with him. He wanted the bike and took it. But I described how he had a long line of ancestors who worked very hard to live righteously and that doing so was not always easy. Living a righteous life is a struggle—one with successes and with failures. Life presents us all with many temptations. When he decided to steal the bike, he disrespected, albeit unintentionally, what those before him had worked so hard for and the values for which they had sacrificed. He jeopardized other members of his identity group to the degree that he helped the "victim" form an opinion about "Jews." He harmed, in a small way, the family name, which has a value derived from real people struggling through life over time in a particular way. Some family names come to represent a history of struggling fairly well—with integrity. Some family names come to stand for selfishness and poor judgment. And some family names stand for very little because there has been no sense of heritage or connectedness tying individuals' lives together.

In a small way, he also hurt himself. He wrote a paragraph in the "long book." It was important for him to know that others had written such paragraphs during their lives—paragraphs about which they were not proud. But I wanted him to know that there were many more paragraphs to come, and that the idea is to help make it the best book possible. Accept human frailties but strive to rise above them. I just wanted him to be conscious of a larger picture than himself and his mother and me.

Believe it or not, all of this is what runs through my head now as I conjure the image of my dog nestled in the grass of my suburban yard seeming to be connecting with his primordial ancestry.

Dog Collar

Ears perked, eyes sparkling,
Alertly snorting the sun,
I cinch the collar around your neck,
And we submit to what must be done.

Reflection on "Dog Collar"

The tension between free will and the rules of civilized living jumped out at me as I performed this simple task of putting a collar on my dog. Social convention (and law) dictated that I keep him on a leash when I took him for a walk. His being and essence of spirit, though, wanted to run free.

This is one of the central dramas of human existence—how does an individual retain and nurture the root of all individuality, namely free will, while making the right and necessary compromises that define civilized living?

The process by which this drama is managed in child-rearing is called socialization. Sometimes it's no big deal. Other times quite different. For example, when I needed to help my children learn how to share toys with other children, a backdrop of righteousness tempered the hassle of doing so. "I know it's an unpleasant lesson to learn, honey, but I also know it's good for you. It's the right way to be." Or, it was clear, though extremely difficult, when I had to force-feed medicine while my child was fighting it tooth and nail. I had confidence that these assaults on free will were justified.

However, when the preschool would insist on my son sitting still during "circle time" (a story time), it became difficult. His "spirit" was to be an active agent in his life and he was curious. He wanted to explore the room and find things of interest. Circle time required him to be a somewhat passive listener. Teachers would say,

"He needs to learn to conform with school rules and routines if he's to do well in school over time."

Our struggle as parents was in how to strike a balance between society's desire and requirement for conformity and the preservation of spirit. We knew that the world will always overstate the requirement for conformity, and we needed to help our child learn how to bend enough to be social, yet not so much as to lose touch with himself or herself. We did not want to raise a perfectly socially appropriate person who was lost in terms of self-knowledge. I thought many times that this must be what horse trainers go through when they are "breaking" a horse while trying to preserve their essential spirit—"break" the horse but don't "break" the spirit.

Errors made in managing this delicate balance have huge human consequences. On one hand, an affronted spirit fights back with a vengeance. Think of all the hostile behavior that reflects the anger and assertiveness of a free will that has been repeatedly threatened and assaulted. People lashing out at others with little or no provocation. People disregarding rules of conduct and laws. This can be the result when the socialization process does not provide an individual enough breathing room for self-expression and self-assertion. That's why giving choices is such an important childrearing practice.

And when a person's spirit is broken, they can become hopeless and helpless. They get depressed. They become automatons going through life with little self-awareness. Or, in the best cases, these are people who go through the motions of life looking quite normal. They do everything they're supposed to do. But they lack passion and creativity. They don't achieve deep love and intimacy. They have an air of superficiality because they dare not dig too deep within themselves. To do so runs the risk of discovering parts of themselves that could make them run amok. Some of these people live their entire lives this way. They die this way. Others have an awakening in midlife when they discover that they did everything right for a long time but it didn't bring satisfaction.

Yes, socialization is a must, but it must be done with respect for the human free will. As adults we are able to impose our will on children by sheer force. This is a power which few know how to use wisely and judiciously. At our best we nurture the free will of our children, teaching them how to make decisions and teaching them what they need to know in order to make good decisions for themselves. But we get so nervous that we won't like their decisions, or we're in such a hurry, that we take over and tell them what to do. We don't exercise enough self-restraint. The wise and judicious exercise of power is one of humanity's greatest challenges.

Success

Timidly climbing this slick rock wall,
My eyes reflexively imagine the fall,
With each step higher the anxiety rises,
So I slip ... to end the suspense.

REFLECTION ON "SUCCESS"

Each step higher in climbing Mt. Achievement is a small success. Each step higher brings you that much closer to the summit and ultimate victory. And for some, success breeds success—meaning with each step they become increasingly emboldened. With each advancement their adrenaline pumps as they see success closer in sight.

For others, though, each step higher calculates as that much farther to fall. With each step comes increasing danger. The tension, for some, becomes unbearable, and so they relieve the tension by failing. It's purposeful but not fully conscious. To observers they just seem to be their own worst enemy.

A young woman whom I saw in therapy inspired this poem. She was in her late 20s and was a waitress at a bar. She was seeing me because she had developed a significant case of bulimia. As I delved into her past, I got the idea that she might have had an undiagnosed learning disability growing up. She went and got tested and found out that indeed she did have a learning disability and undoubtedly did as a child as well. This diagnosis opened up a complete new understanding of her life and herself.

She had struggled terribly in school, with the result being that she came to believe that she was "stupid." She made a number of attempts to go to college but each time quit. She made a few attempts to get "real jobs" (as she would call them), but also quit these. Then this new light bulb went off. "Maybe I'm not stupid, but actually smart with a learning disability. Maybe I am a capable person."

So, she reentered college, only this time hooked in with the special needs program. Tests were read to her and she could dictate her answers. Readers recorded her textbook assignments so she could listen to the chapters instead of reading them. She began her ascent. But her mind had been trained to expect failure. So with each step higher, her anxiety intensified. Though she was succeeding, she expected to ultimately fall. My job was to help her manage her anxiety—to help her confidence build upon her successes.

She earned A's in every course she took. We began to turn the corner in terms of her expectations. She began to gain confidence with each success. Fretting became replaced by excitement and boundless energy. She burst forth! It was like watching time-lapse photography of a flower blooming. She began to write for the school newspaper. She became involved in student government. She began tutoring others. She graduated and then entered an MBA program. It was a truly amazing transformation to facilitate and to witness.

Potential can be a blessing and can also be a burden. It depends on how fearful one is of failure. If failure is FAILURE—that is, a judgment of your entire being and worth—then the ascent of Mt. Achievement is riddled with constant anxiety. If, on the other hand, failure is a stumble—something you get up from and leave behind— something as natural as rain … then potential feels like your favorite sweatshirt and jeans. You love being in it.

Talking

The thought just formed, so freshly born,
Was snatched by my tongue and altered,
And then thrust out, for you to know about,
But on meaning-bent wings it faltered.

REFLECTION ON "TALKING"

I have had so much disappointment and frustration with my words not being received as they were intended. While I may think that I have a clear thought conveyed clearly by the words I select and my manner of delivering them, they inevitably are sifted through the filters people have for making sense of their world. We develop filters to hear what we want or expect to hear. Here's a small example. It was a time of the day to take the dog for a walk. My wife and I have been trying to do that together. I initiated the suggestion of "Let's take the dog for a walk." For good reasons of her own, she didn't feel like doing it. She said, "Let's wait until it's warmer." From past experience, I knew that "later" was not likely to arrive. I thought she was just tired and "later" would run up against dinner time and then never arrive. I said, "No worries. I'll take him now." She interpreted that I was disappointed with her and possibly upset, even though I wasn't. We both had words running through filters, creating a subtextual conversation that created confusion and miscommunication. This kind of thing happens often. Thankfully we have a strong relationship, and miscues like that vanish into nothingness. But sometimes this kind of miscommunication carries a wallop of hurt feelings and frustration. And in more superficially connected work and social relationships, those miscommunications can make lasting impressions, usually negative and sometimes positive.

Alternatively, there are the times when I cannot find words to express what I want. They turn the profound into the mundane, elegance into clumsiness, and enlightenment into stone-like thuds. Many times that happens when I'm asked about what I think of a person, a rich experience, or simply "What are you feeling?" I get stuck in trying to find the right words to express myself and default to the adolescent anthem "I don't know." Instead of struggling and fumbling my way through weak efforts to assemble some kind of response, I fall silent, leaving the well-intentioned listener empty-handed. I wish I could do better, and I feel bad when the person I leave hanging is my wife. Thankfully, sometimes, being the exquisite empath she is, she derives the answer more telepathically.

More generally, I think of the heart-hurt that comes when we all are talking *at* each other and not doing a great job of listening. We all want to be heard, understood, and accepted even if there is disagreement. But, when we don't feel heard, we either shut down or talk louder and longer, which often shuts down listeners even more. It becomes a no-win scenario of "listen to me, I have something I want you to understand" … "No, you listen to me, I have something *I* want *you* to understand" … "No, not until you listen to me first" … "Over my dead body. You listen to me first." Standoffs with pejorative attributions toward one another splatter on the paths we are walking.

I have found that, with exceptions, the implicit cultural agreement of "reciprocity" can be counted on. If I offer the gift of listening to someone, it is more likely they will respond in kind *at some point*. There's not much risk, for if reciprocity is not forthcoming, I have given a gift that cost me very little after I set aside foolish pride. Gift giving is good as an act of love. And love breeds love.

Reacting

As the ball collides with the concrete floor,
It absorbs the shock and then evens the score,
By pushing back with an equal force.
Bouncing imprisoned on its freedom course.

REFLECTION ON "REACTING"

When I was a teenager in the '60s I wore my hair longer than my parents liked. I believed that people should be valued based on their character and actions and not on more superficial qualities such as their appearance. And, so, my hair was a statement of that value and an assertion of being different from my parents' generation. Each year I would find myself in the midst of a muggy Midwest summer and would, from time to time, want to cut my bushy hair for relief. I could get as far as making an appointment to get my hair cut, and then, invariably, my father would make some comment about my hair that I heard as sarcastic or disparaging. That threw me into a predicament. I could go ahead with my plan to get my hair cut, *but,* then it felt like I was simply caving in to his pressures. My prideful sense of autonomy made resisting him more important than the summertime comfort I might achieve.

Who was controlling whom? I wanted my hair cut, but I didn't do it. *He was in control.* He wanted my hair cut and I didn't do it. *I was in control.* We were both in control, *and* we were both not in control. I felt that paradox but didn't understand it.

Some people argue that free will is simply an illusion and that every decision we make is inevitable based on the totality of influences up to that point. Did I choose to keep my hair long or was that choice inevitable ... destined to be based on my personality and history with my father? I can understand that as a philosophical argument, but practically I think with each decision we make that we really do have the capacity to select one way or another. The importance to me of self-determination, along with feeling the uncomfortable paradox inside of me, kept me struggling until I came to an understanding that each choice I made was indeed a *choice* that *I* was determining. Using the adolescent hair example, if I got my hair cut, it was because I wanted my hair shorter, and my father's reaction was a separate matter. I came to a point where if my father was pleased with my choices, I could feel good in terms of being a son who was satisfying his father, and if my father was displeased with my choices, I could accept that as well. If I had the desire to show my father that I was my own person and not just a person conforming to what others wanted, the best way to do that was to stay in touch with my inner voice and act accordingly. Sometimes I'd be in sync with others and sometimes not, but at least I would have lived *my* life.

As it turned out, I worked for about 20 years with my father in his business. At first I was afraid to do it, because I wasn't confident that I could find a good resolution to this dilemma of differentiating between whether what I was doing was what I freely chose versus a gradual and insidious loss of self resulting from yielding to his influence. My intuition told me that facing the fear and the challenge would be important for my journey of self-development, and so I jumped in. I am so grateful that I did, for the experience brought me and my father closer and helped me mature in my own development.

Civilized

Motionless, with grace supporting her wings,
The pelican hovers as the sunset sings,
Then she swiftly strikes from her lofty height,
And I stumble through my jumble of
wrong and right.

Reflection on "Civilized"

Like all animals, we kill to survive. We kill other animals and we kill plants. I can recall being about ten years old and wondering why people seemed to place higher value on animal life than the lives of plants. Life seemed to be a precious miracle, no matter its form. My poor mother endured many conversations on that topic—for example, I would provoke her by asking why is it any sadder or more wrong to snatch a cucumber from its lifeline and shorten its natural life cycle than to do the same with an animal or person? My mother was very tolerant.

The morality of killing seems to be about its necessity. Was the killing for survival? Or was it for sport, an expression of anger or hatred, paranoia, exaggerated perceptions of threat ... that is, for reasons detached from actual survival? When killing for nutritional sustenance, animals seem to do so dispassionately. When killing to protect territory or their social status, it seems more violent to me. Humans seem to misappropriate violence more than other species—taking aggressiveness to the point of morally offensive vulgarity. We perceive levels of threat that are derived more from insecurities and fear than from the actual threat at hand. With the "uncoveries" of the universal character strengths by the field of positive psychology (check out www.viacharacter.org), we now know we possess tools for bending the arc of human development toward our highest promise, in which we are able to pursue our potentials without unnecessarily diminishing the opportunities for other people and species to do the same. Here's to putting our shoulders to the task of beginning the bending!

PART TWO

Expressions of Love

Problems

When problems arise
In your eyes
I see you
Leave me alone.

REFLECTION ON "PROBLEMS"

Truth has a way of showing up unannounced on your doorstep. "Surprise! I'm here to rock your world now!" And when that truth is about a problem in a relationship, such as a violation of trust, it's often delivered by someone's eyes. When you look directly into your lover's eyes and see trouble, there's no playing around. Truth makes its entrance like John Wayne throwing open the swinging doors of a saloon. It makes its appearance like a lightning bolt striking in the jet-black night. It stops your heart. Your blood runs cold. There's no hiding. All games come to a halt. Suddenly there's trouble in paradise. You're in the room with "the beast," and it commands full attention.

What do you do? Face it directly—head-on? Or run and hide? My instincts tell me to run and hide if I can. I am very uncomfortable with conflict. So, I tend to withdraw by building a wall around my emotions and refusing to talk much. I see the issue at hand and hope, even demand, to be left alone.

When I am in that self-imposed isolation, I have mixed feelings—vulnerability *and* strength. On one hand there is fear and panic in my aloneness and impotence. And guilt from understanding how the other person has been impacted, while at the same time not conveying that understanding as I flee the scene. But, I also gain a sense of strength that comes with my skills for protecting myself. I am mighty in my armor!

My tendency to stuff my feelings and to hope problems disappear has always been unacceptable to my wife. She is a Truth seeker. She sees the problems in my eyes. And she sees me retreat, leaving *her* all alone. I hate it when I do this, because I see her hurt and her sense of abandonment. She has worked on me for many years to talk things out with her instead of retreating. She has taught me to stand in the face of Truth—to be a different kind of warrior ... to summon courage. I am indebted to her for being such a determined teacher, and sorry I have not been a better student.

Despair

Circle fragments float like grins,
Mocking, along with violins,
My life, which has gone amiss.
Blown apart by a kiss.

REFLECTION ON "DESPAIR"

Sexual infidelities are such dangerous liaisons. History has proven that in the multitude of tragic stories fueled by the sexual drive. The lure of a woman's lips. Crossing a forbidden sexual barrier. It's magnetic. It's so charged—the charges attracting one another until the moment of choice presents itself. One step forward and the boundary is crossed. The taboo gets shattered. There is no *return*, really, just *another* turn. The boundary-crossing kiss can have such a big price that goes along with it. The price and warning are usually not well labeled. It's in very small print—small enough to be overlooked.

Then a chain of events grabs you like a current accelerating you toward the dangerous waterfall. Hiding and secrecy cause suspicion and guilt. Victimhood fuels anger that explodes destructively. Then the desperate and clingy attempts to hold on ... to rewind ... to reconstruct. Finally, the pieces can't come back together. All the king's horses, and all the king's men, can't put Humpty together again. The demise. Left alone. No spouse. No lover. No friend. No one. Having blown it. Having thrown it all away. Five, four, three, two, one ... KISS ... engines ignite ... launched into the cold, deep darkness of aloneness.

Affair

Though I know it's not right,
I must start a fight,
To get time alone,
For passion on the phone.

Time Alone

A little fight might do the trick,
He'll poke and I'll pick,
I'll cry, and he'll groan,
Then, at last, time alone.

Reflection on "Affair" ... "Time Alone"

One of the first things I learned as a psychotherapist is to *follow the behaviors* more than *follow the words*. What is someone *doing* as opposed to what they are *saying* about what they do?

A couple would come into my office and complain about fighting. They would say they fight about finances, or irresponsibility, or childrearing, or whatever their fighting words might be about. As a psychotherapist, it was usually helpful to tune out the words and focus instead on behavior. He did this, then she did that, and then ... and then. Look at the chain of behaviors. "Actions speak louder than words." It was always important to keep extending my questioning about "and then," because sometimes the truth was hiding down the chain of events, behind one more question of "And then?"

Often the underlying purpose of offensive behaviors is the regulation of personal space. We all have times when we just want some space and times when we want connection. For couples, there are necessarily times when one person is seeking connection when the other is desiring space. We can't always be in sync. Convention has it that asserting the desire for space is rude in romantic relationships as it is interpreted as a lack of love. The assumption that "Since we love each other, we should always want to be together with each other" is a false and destructive belief. So, partners discover ways to push each other away with offensive behavior. It's a subconscious process.

132

Other times the source of couples' fighting is a sexual attraction and infatuation with a third person. Forbidden attraction makes us crazy. Lust and desire can drive us to do things we know aren't right. We become highly excited, obsessive, and driven, against the hidden backdrop of guilt. Instincts take over. Our sense of right and wrong can become blurred. Our moral compass stops working. We subconsciously create fights that give us the space for the liaison. A common defense strategy against feeling guilt is to deflect it away from oneself by directing it outward as anger, irritation, or hate—to spouses, children, friends, and others. Freud observed the process of guilt-turning-to-anger about 150 years ago.

Ironically, the ensuing fight often baits the "victimized" partner into misbehaving, thus creating a useful distraction. The offending partner can actually get up in arms about things their partner said and did during the fight, moving the focus away from their own misdeeds. It all becomes an emotional tornado in which rationality has little chance.

So it goes. Time and time again. The couple fights or just drifts apart. One person knows why. The other remains in the dark. Until, at some point, Truth reveals itself as it always does, and then everything falls apart. The fog of intrigue, lust, subterfuge and confusion clears, leaving just pain.

As if this is not a sordid enough pattern that all too many couples find themselves playing out, sometimes an insidious fuel gets added to the fire. After they would argue, get some time apart, and one partner would squeeze in a secret liaison, the couple would make up with amazing hot lovemaking. Talk about conditioned behavior! Infidelity, deception, and obnoxious behavior being reinforced with one of the most intense pleasures possible. No wonder the pattern becomes hard to break!

Evening Gown

"Why are you shouting at me?"
I cried as I crumbled down.
I don't want to fight ... especially tonight,
In my pretty new evening gown.

REFLECTION ON "EVENING GOWN"

In this scene, a couple is getting ready for a special event. Formalwear and fantasy. Cinderella and the prince at the ball. A break in the humdrum of life. Romance. With little-girl fantasies swirling in her head she puts on her evening gown and her makeup and puts her hair up. Her body tingles and she twirls to her own delight. She's ready for good-time retreat from her everyday responsibilities.

And then … WHAM! Reality bites. Her husband lashes out. Maybe he's upset that his cummerbund only fits tightly now due to weight gain. Maybe he asked her to pick up his other shirt and she forgot. Maybe he's feeling like a loser. Maybe he's anxious about the event itself. Who knows? But the beast comes out and shatters everything with a snide or harsh comment. The damage is done. The fight is on. She has the wind knocked out of her by this shot to her solar plexus.

There's no recovery for the time being. For it takes some time to get lulled back into the hypnotic state where we can pretend with ourselves that we are safe from the randomness of life and where everything is as it should be. We love our retreats from reality when we can simply relax … ease up. But, harsh reality never stops nipping at the heels. And it can attack at the most inopportune times! We go back and forth between illusion and reality. For now, the night has been shattered for this woman.

Life intrudes on so many hopes and expectations. A wedding celebration shattered by the discovery of an affair. A romantic night with your spouse ruined by an argument. A birthday card not received. A weekend interrupted by a family or work emergency. So it goes. We get disappointed. Then recover. Get knocked down again. Recover. So much of life seems to be about the recovery. Resilience.

Cold Coffee

She reached with desire,
Hope made her able.
His stillness left her gazing at
Cold coffee on the table.

REFLECTION ON "COLD COFFEE"

Sometimes love can grow so cold. Like two objects drawn quickly together only to bounce off each other in slow motion. Lovers come together like an atomic fusion. Then, gradually they can drift apart, until at some point they feel the coldness of disconnection.

Here a husband and wife lie next to each other in bed. They haven't been fighting. They've just been distant from each other lately. The husband is feigning sleep to avoid the potential pain of a hollow or a hurtful conversation. I am sad and embarrassed to reflect on how many times I have been the pretender in this scene. Unless someone makes a move to close the gap, it might just keep widening to a point of no return.

But reaching out is a risk. The possibility of rejection creates vulnerability. In this instance the wife, bolstered by a flash of hope lighting up the darkness of loneliness, reaches out tentatively toward her husband's back, which is facing her. She gently touches him on the shoulder hoping he will roll over and reciprocate. Not for sex ... just to make contact. To heal the laceration of disconnection. But he remains still. He can't move past his hurt and pride, instead remaining locked in position. The lack of response does not surprise her ... just disappoints. Its familiarity results in a thud instead of a sharp pain.

She gets out of bed, too disturbed to sleep, and goes into the kitchen—the place of self-nurturing. The place of shared meals and conversation. As she slumps into the chair at the kitchen table she stares ahead and sees a cup of cold coffee on the table. It seems so apropos. "How did it come to this?" she wonders. "How can I reel him back?" "Why am I always the one who has to reach out and bridge the void?" It's just too much to keep thinking about. So, she grabs the crossword puzzle until she can fall asleep.

While I am sorry for the times when my cowardice has constructed a brick wall and inflicted deep pain, I am still prone to hide and leave my wife in the cold. She ultimately bridges the gap and pulls me back to my love. I am grateful for her courage and commitment. And I am astonished and freaked out how the warm sunshine of our love can so quickly and surprisingly turn to a dark, cold void. I don't understand.

Dining Together

Dining at the kitchen table,
Denying our state of smother,
The TV takes away the pain,
Of looking at one another.

Routinized

The smile, the heart-jump, the child-zeal,
That sizzled between our souls,
Routinized so subtly,
Sad anesthetic feel.

REFLECTION ON "DINING TOGETHER"
... "ROUTINIZED"

It's so painful to be in a dying relationship. Unlike relationships that have already died and the people have moved on, dying relationships are marked by muffled agony. It is heartbreaking as relationships stay together despite the fact that their life force has dwindled to almost nothing. To me it's like watching an animal suffer. Caught in the jaws of a trapper's trap. Writhing in pain. Unable to release itself or end the suffering of the entrapment. That's what happens to many couples.

They begin their relationship with energy. Over time their growth curves as individuals flatten. They come to know just about everything about one another. The interest of discovering and being discovered has dwindled. The recurring problems have been beaten to death. Conversations have been repeated one too many times. The flame flickers. Curiosity no longer drives new discovery.

But neither person has the courage, or sometimes even the insight, to call it out for what it is. Some relationship is better than nothing ... than being alone. So, couples stay together in denied agony for fear of loneliness and change. To accomplish this, each partner needs to chew off a body part to escape the trap. Maybe friendships drift away. Maybe their precious sense of humor disappears. Maybe their compassion retreats.

Hearts harden. Each, now missing essential parts of themselves, ironically leans on the other as they hobble here and there. They become bound by fear and desperation. Resentment is often the backdrop on which the relationship then plays itself out.

I have worried about arriving at this place sometime in my life and have felt it coming and going. I specifically recall a time when my wife and I were on vacation in England and I felt so distant from her that I was fairly certain that our relationship was over. I felt dark and cold as we awoke in the country manor and gazed upon a romantic, morning-mist-filled field. That morning was filled with mourning. I felt helpless in the presence of this assertive dark force that came out of nowhere. I do not recall how we crawled out of that abyss. I suspect it may have started by my wife reaching out to hold my hand as we walked down a cobblestone street in a quaint old town. When she does that, it seems to say to me, "Come on. Remember? We love each other. We're best friends." I go along with that, holding the hope that the physical connection will stoke my body memory.

I am afraid of getting stuck there sometime. I take reassurance in my belief that my wife wouldn't allow us to be lifeless together for too long. One way or another, she would heal us or let us go to grow.

Deciding

I decide, right or wrong,
And then take what comes along.
Can't stand to do as you,
And think, think, think it through.

REFLECTION ON "DECIDING"

As I have probably conveyed already, my wife is a person of action. She hates to sit on anxiety or guilt or any "negative" emotion that she thinks might be able to be resolved. Lingering feelings like that create an uneasy feeling. The *un*ease registers as if it's a *dis*ease. In such instances she moves pretty quickly and deliberately to cure the "illness" … to put a quick end to the emotional discomfort that accompanies uncertainty.

On the other hand, my upbringing and constitution have conditioned me to have relatively great tolerance for hovering in a state of uncertainty. I was raised in a family that readily noticed mistakes. I can remember proudly bringing my father pieces of my handiwork that I had put much effort into, only to have him notice something I had ignored or done wrong. I distinctly recall holding forth a model car that I had glued together. I thought it looked so cool—and I made it all by myself! As I recall, Dad said "Nice job" and then quickly pointed out how sloppily I had applied the glue. And, I recall family members catching any little mistake I might make in speaking or based in lacking knowledge and jumping all over me with ridicule. It was not a picking on *me* in particular. It was just part of our family culture.

As a result, I grew to be very vigilant about avoiding mistakes. Most every decision, from ordering a meal at a restaurant to buying a couch to deciding to have children became a rather torturous process inflicted by the insistent drive to avoid making a mistake. It's like my psyche developed Doberman Pinscher guard dogs to constantly pace back and forth to warn me of encroaching errors. My dreams reflect this kind of constitutional worry, being full of stories where I've messed up in a dumbfounding and inexplicable way. I have envied my good friend whose dreams are full of pleasant fantasy. Wow. That would be fun. I even have an eerie and disquieting facility to see typographical errors in manuscripts and wrong numbers in spreadsheets. My critical thinking is one of my great assets while at the same time being one of my greatest liabilities.

Our different decision-making styles have caused my wife and I to experience our share of strife when decisions need to be mutually agreed upon. Once we got over being annoyed with our different styles, we realized that together we are able to arrive at something resembling a reasonable decision-making process. Individually we each may be a bit skewed. But together we create a good balance. Our differences actually can lead to improved decisions, though they almost always involve some tension.

When we were buying our first home, we were each anxious. She was anxious to get a home, furnish it, and start a new chapter. I was anxious about making a big mistake. I noticed that we ended up taking on roles. Since I was being a bit hypercritical, she was becoming a bit more blindly optimistic as a correction to my negativity. "I smelled mildew in the basement and worry there might be a problem with the foundation." "I'm sure it is fine, and if not, we can fix it easily." Her blind faith moved me to become more worried and critical. As I moved more in that direction, she moved more toward wishful thinking. I took on the role of "Look how much water is missing from the glass" and she took the role of "Look how much water is in the glass." If either of us were making the decision alone instead of as a couple, we might have been more balanced. But, together, we pushed each other into *roles*—the optimist vs. the pessimist. In general, the more extreme one member of a couple becomes, the more it behooves the other to exaggerate themselves in order to provide counterbalance. This is a disservice of complementary relationships. We can lose our completeness as individuals since all that comes to matter is that the partners, as a unit, have between them the qualities and characteristics necessary to function well.

This kind of complementarity in relationships works best if we can grow from *counterbalancing* to *emulating* the other. So, instead of "I'll act the pessimist and you'll act the optimist," it can become "I will focus more on the positives and you will acknowledge more of the negatives." At this point in my relationship with my wife, I think we are growing toward and with one another more than when we were younger and exaggerating our differences.

Departure

They tightly hugged,
And privately whispered,
Then parted ...
Gently weeping.

REFLECTION ON "DEPARTURE"

I watch people closely. I enjoy it. It's completely engaging for me. My watching is not particularly purposeful. I'm not so much studying people for anything in particular as much as just looking. I find body language interesting—averting eyes belying nervousness, stiff gaits of people tightly in control, attitude emanating from a swagger, a smile effortfully stretching against tension, a face touch indicating unease, reaching for a drink for reasons other than thirst. I can literally spend hours at a time just watching people do "their dance."

This poem is self-descriptive and is one of many "snapshots" taken while waiting at an airport. There was so much love in this departure scene. The hug was warm, not desperate. The weeping was that weird mixture of worry and anticipated loss that only occurs with someone you love and care deeply about.

This poem reminds me of times when I have decided to end the suffering of my dogs. The last time was so painful. First, I have loved every one of my dogs (except one, I must admit) very deeply. Very deeply. Mugsy was a feisty boxer. Boxers have this amazingly zestful personality and, unfortunately, a propensity for cancer. He had an operation for cancer but was getting sick again. The vet told me that he was bleeding internally and that surgery could stem the flow only until the growing cancer would fairly quickly create another bleed. He was lying on his side, tuckered out, as energy drained from him. I looked him in the eyes for a long time before deciding the best course of action was to let him go. He trusted me, and I needed to exercise my best judgment for him. That judgment—of life vs. death—is simply beyond me. I felt that I should not make such a decision. That is a decision for Nature. But, I knew that he depended on me to do what was best for him. And prolonged suffering did not feel right. He needed me to decide.

I did not let him see me cry. I did not want to scare him or worry him. After he passed, I bawled. My heart broke. A year and a half later my heart, which was on the mend, shattered when my father died of cancer. I could not bear the thought of more hurt. But my wife knew that what my heart needed was to be revived with love.

So, about six months after my father passed away, she convinced me to follow her instinct to get a new dog … a new boxer puppy. She was right. He got my heart pumping again. If not for him, I fear that my heart would have kept crusting over gradually, like barnacles accumulating layer by layer on a wharf post. I know my heart has hardened with scars from injuries over time. I fear the loss of my best buddy as he begins to gray. I know my challenge at this point in my life is to keep stretching my heart and trying to keep it pliable.

Husband

"My husband will be by," the old woman said,
Declining the stranger's aid,
While knowing instead that for years he's
been dead,
She survives alone and afraid.

Reflection on "Husband"

The world is a dangerous place. I remember being shocked to the point of near trauma in reading the book and viewing the movie *In Cold Blood*. The title says it all. Horrendous acts of violence against Innocents. I was a young teenager at the time, and my newly developing ability to comprehend such things wrapped around this discovery with fascination and dread. I felt so vulnerable. At any time, for no reason, I could be minding my own business and a stranger could pull me into their nightmare. I felt this when I went to sleep at night in my comfy suburban bed and felt it when I was camping in the wilderness far away from cities and people. Like any fear, it followed me like a shadow. Oh, how sheltered my life was while growing up.

What I was to find out as I grew older was that this was but one of a number of vulnerabilities, which would become a fact of my life. To love my wife and dedicate my life to her was to make myself vulnerable to losing her for any number of reasons. To have children and experience the deep love that is attendant to parenthood is to be as emotionally vulnerable as I can imagine.

In parenting, though, in addition to being vulnerable to random acts of others or Fate, one plays an active role in managing risk. Parenting is, in fact, largely a matter of risk management—judging your child's readiness to venture forward, helping prepare them for these ventures, and then allowing them to venture out where real risk exists. From letting them fall on their face when they're learning to walk, to crossing the street, to staying overnight at a friend's house, to driving a car. The list goes on and on. Our main role as parents is to ready our kids for these ventures and risks, and then to let them go.

The result is that parenting is anxiety provoking. And people have their differing ways of managing this anxiety—from overprotectiveness ("I won't let you get hurt"), to negligence ("I don't care"), to denial of the risks ("Ignorance is bliss"), to prematurely demanding adultlike behaviors from children ("Grow up so I don't have to worry as much"), to self-medicating with alcohol and drugs ("This is all too much for me").

So, our lives are filled with hazard. In this poem an elderly woman who lost her husband years ago knows the dangers lurking around for an elderly single woman like herself. She has had to figure ways to protect herself. One thing she does is to use her husband in death as he served in life—as her protector. Her phone number is still listed in his name. Her subscriptions are in his name. His tools are prominently displayed in the garage for all to see each time she raises the garage door. She is brave and cunning, as she needs to be. Like a pioneer woman whose husband is gone on a long hunting and trapping trip, she must "hold down the fort" however she can.

Then grace enters the picture. A young man, observing her struggle to pull her garbage cans to the street, offers his assistance. Philanthropy—love of mankind.

Altruism. Kindness. Compassion. Goodness reaches out to her in this young man's offer. And the door is slammed shut on it. "My husband will be by" she informs him, just in case he had something else in mind. In case he was the proverbial wolf in sheep's clothing. It works! He walks on. Fear once again rebuffs Love.

I ache over the fears that invade us all and over these lost battles where Fear overcomes Goodness. I swell with pride at our best struggles—those characterized by courage and dignity. And I hope to the point of belief that, though many battles are lost, Love and Goodness will ultimately prevail. We have many capacities for virtuous action. We just need to more consciously and deliberately exercise them.

Indebted

You bend and bend and accommodate,
The debt I accept and accumulate,
And my discontent gets silenced.
Your niceness feels like violence.

REFLECTION ON "INDEBTED"

How can niceness come to feel like violence? Start with a person who has never been in a relationship with a "nice" partner. It might be a woman who has always managed to be with men who are inconsiderate and who put their needs ahead of hers. So, here she finally finds someone "different." He brings her flowers, does the dishes, and opens the door for her, etc. A real gentleman. Or so it appears. She feels so appreciative.

Now for the other ingredient. Reciprocity.

He has grown to understand niceness as a *currency*. When you give something, you're supposed to get something in return. Niceness, for him, is not simply a gift of one's heart ... an act of love. Instead, it is an advance payment—a deposit—on something yet to be specified. But when he decides what he wants, in his mind he is owed big-time. He has already paid. So when he wants to have sex, or wants his sex this way or that, or wants her to entertain his friends, or wants her to dress a certain way and wear her hair a certain way, or to limit her contact with her friends and wait at home for him, it is something he *deserves*. Whatever it is, he is owed. He prepaid.

So, here are two people. One is "a nice guy" who thinks his niceness earns him favor. He is unaware of his ulterior motives or his assumptions about reciprocity. The other is a woman who buys into it. Yes, she *should* return the favor. After a while, she can't figure out why she's so unhappy. She feels guilty for being unhappy. On the surface this guy seems so different from the others. He's so nice. She should be appreciative. She should be happy. She thinks there must be something wrong with her. The vicious cycle begins spinning faster. Something is wrong with her, he acts nicely, she feels undeserving, he tries harder by giving more, she feels worse, and he becomes angry. She doesn't understand the resentment riding beneath her sense of obligation.

But, in time, she realizes that he's not giving freely but with strings attached. His niceness is just a different version of the self-centeredness that she is all too familiar with. Each time he gives, the weight of obligation gets heavier. A different form of manipulation and coercion. He is clueless. He thinks he's just being a really nice guy. On the surface it's befuddling to both parties and it's why folks like these commonly found themselves in my psychotherapy office.

Expectations from others can feel like coercion.

Mourning

Richly lost in love was I,
With my daughter—how we'd laugh and cry,
Then she died ... and all my blood did drain,
Leaving me cold at her grave ... in the rain.

Organ Donor

In my womb, now a tomb,
Rests my child without her brain,
Waiting to part with her soul and heart,
As I reason with my pain.

Reflection on "Mourning" ... "Organ Donor"

The unthinkable. Losing a child. Attending the funeral described in "Mourning" was one of the saddest events of my life. The parents were acquaintances of mine. One day the mother and her two-year-old daughter were touring the construction going on in their new house. The daughter was saddled on her mother's hip. Then a leaning stack of drywall tipped the wrong way and fell on top of them, crushing the toddler to death.

It rained the day she was buried. How apt. Her older sister requested that everyone sing "Silent Night." It was nearly too much to bear.

"Organ Donor" was stimulated by an article I read in the newspaper. A woman learned that the child she was carrying had an essentially empty skull. The brain was not going to grow. I shudder to think of her receiving that news.

And then, her decision to keep her pregnancy going—carrying a child who she would never hold and nurture. Instead she was growing organs for the doctors to harvest to give to others in need. A desperate and valiant effort to find meaning in her tragedy. I imagined the many times she must have reasoned her way through the pain of her bizarre circumstance. Human virtue shining in the abyss of darkness.

Having children of my own, this entire topic is one at which I can hardly glance.

I recall a 3 a.m. phone call in which the caller stated my son's name and inquired as to whether she was in fact speaking to his father. "He has been in a serious car accident and he asked me to call you. The accident was on Reading Road." The blood drained from my body. My wife was by that time sitting up in bed alarmed and waiting to hear from me what the bad news was. We hurriedly jumped into our car to get to the scene of the accident, only to realize we hadn't been told where on the very lengthy Reading Road the accident had occurred. While I'm guessing where it might have happened, my wife is on the phone frantically calling police departments until we manage to arrive at the scene of the accident. I see lights flashing and emergency medical personnel leaning over a motionless person. I see the person's feet and realize it's my son. Not knowing what carnage I might encounter, I suggested to my wife that she stay in the car, and I ran over to where he was. My first relief was to see that he was conscious and that it wasn't a bloody scene. Then a major second infusion of relief when I was told he didn't seem to have any broken bones or head trauma, and the person in the other car was not badly hurt. I jumped in the ambulance with my son while my wife followed to the hospital, where he was cleared of internal bleeding. Death brushed by us that day, leaving us alone. I have kept the shoes I was wearing that night as a reminder of life's tenuousness, of the importance of showing love and appreciating my many blessings.

To love is to become vulnerable.

Shallow Creek

Shallow creek, you hurt my feet,
You are refreshing and sweet to drink,
But your rocks so close to your top,
Cut my soles and make me bleed.

Loud Man

As the loud man
Merely spoke to his daughter,
I knew ...
She didn't like him.

REFLECTION ON "SHALLOW CREEK" ... "LOUD MAN"

I n the dance of social interaction, some people glide like Fred Astaire with Ginger Rogers (I don't know a contemporary paradigmatic dance couple). Others, lacking the intuition and sensitivity to their partner, are klutzes. They are the proverbial "bull in a china shop" or the "guy with two left feet." Not meaning ill, they knock people over.

Here that person is a father. Nearly everything about him is LOUD—meaning it is not modulated for the particular person or situation. He comes in one form and one form only. What you see is what you get. Straight up. No nuances. No adjustment to others' moods or to circumstances.

He thinks he's a great dad. He loves his daughter, goes to her school events, attends her soccer games, buys her a car, provides a nice home and a private school, and so on and so on. But he's LOUD. And she doesn't like that about him. She bears the emotional bruises of his clumsiness. She needs some sensitivity. She needs Fred Astaire—a dad who can lead but at the same time be responsive to her. She needs someone to listen and not just tell her. From time to time she needs a hug and reassurance in lieu of a motivational speech.

But we don't choose our parents. A parent might be more transactional and pragmatic in their approach to their life, while a child may be more emotionally sensitive and philosophical. This is portrayed in the poem "Shallow Creek."

In "Loud Man," the daughter got Mr. Loud as her dad. And she doesn't like it. She doesn't like him—her own dad. I know that must have been a deep struggle. A child *is supposed to* love their father, especially one who is a good father, so I guess she probably denied her dislike. I can imagine so many downstream problems she'll experience just based on that denial. I predict confusing unhappiness in marriage or partnering.

My heart went out to them both as I stood nearby and thought of how parent-child personality differences can interfere with a level of closeness that both child and parent deeply desire. I admire those who manage to bridge the gaps of their differences with love and affection.

Childhood

"I had my horse and my dog," he explained,

About surviving the buried years,

When arms were swinging and mouths
were yelling,

And heads had wooden ears.

REFLECTION ON "CHILDHOOD"

THIS poem brings me great pain. A child ... so innocent ... subjected to all sorts of mayhem created by adults who considered him nothing much more than an appendage. This was the childhood of a college professor who was a patient of mine. His mother was distant and self-absorbed. His father was a workaholic and alcoholic. When asked to recall his best memories of being with his father, he recounted sitting on his father's lap, playing with his big hands, with the sweet stench of whiskey enveloping him. It was a bittersweet memory, because while remembering how special that attention was to him at the time, he could see from his adult vantage point how pathetic it was. He could see how his father's alcoholism was the source of so much pain and suffering in his household.

His childhood was not only marked by invisibility, it was also filled with adults arguing and fighting. To deaden the fear and pain of observing all of this, he depersonalized it. It was as if the mouths which were yelling and the arms that were hitting were not parts of real people, but almost like objects flying around propelled by psychokinetic energy. And when he would cry or pray for help, his cries and prayers fell on deaf ears.

Thankfully, he had some animals in his life—a dog and a horse—which could be his friends. He played with them. He talked to them and he thought they listened compassionately. He cuddled and snuggled with them.

They were his only source of comfort, and with them he was at ease. They helped him survive. Indeed, the picture of his childhood was very sad.

Pets play an amazing role in our lives. More than two out of three households in the U.S. have a pet! Sixty-eight percent as of 2018. That says something! Pets tend to be sources of unconditional love … in both directions. In our caring for them we find meaning and purpose. I don't know if there are other examples of cross-species intimate relationships in the animal kingdom, but I am amazed at our cross-species relationships. I am certainly very grateful for these relationships in my life. I am confident that my oxytocin flows, as does his, as my dog and I snuggle together.

Baby in Bed

I hear you squeal in utter delight,
As balloon bouquets dance in your sight,
Melting doves rise toward heaven,
As I eavesdrop at your door.

Daughter Love

I'm bound to you in daughter love,
Muscle jungle baby dove,
Lying next to me in bliss,
High-rising helium hearts.

Tiny Tot

Tiny tot can't do a thing,
Lying helpless and babbling.
I'm bonded to you and by this love bound,
And so bound I am to feel bossed around.

REFLECTION ON "BABY IN BED" …
"TINY TOT"

"Baby in Bed" expresses one of the pure joys of having an infant—cooing. As irritating as crying can be, cooing is the opposite. There was nothing … literally nothing … in my experience that was like a baby—my baby—cooing. I would typically feed her a bottle and then put her to bed. The feeding would set the mood. Cradling my hungry baby in my arms and then giving her a bottle of nutrition was such a deeply satisfying experience. She latched on to the nipple and immediately entered a state of pure, unadulterated bliss.

After feeding, the two of us would float up the stairs in shared euphoria and I would place her in her crib. Above her crib was a mobile with different colored balloons. I'd lay her down ever so gently so as not to shatter her precious and fragile state of being. Then, like Muhammad Ali floating across the canvas, or Michael Jackson moonwalking, I would make every effort to glide silently to the doorway and make my exit. This particular time, as I squeezed the door shut, I heard her cooing at the balloons. The "heroin" (oxytocin) hit my brain and I stood there, high as a kite, listening. It felt like we were rising toward heaven together on our own private amusement ride.

"Daughter Love" is in a similar vein, conveying the richly textured experience of being a father who was in it with both feet—the struggles and joys of living and growing and the critical responsibility I felt, given my bond with her. Visceral. Physical. Primordial. Peaceful.

"Tiny Tot" expresses the duality of the romanticized experience of bonding. That is, while bonding to a child was awesome, there was a dimension of imprisonment in being bonded to another person—especially one who was young and helpless. The extreme satisfaction of "being one" with another juxtaposed against the discomfort which accompanied my loss of freedom resulting from my own sense of duty and responsibility. It created a strange brew. At times the "calls to duty" seemed like responding to a drill sergeant—"Yes sir, sir. I'll get on that right away!" as I ran to warm a bottle or replace a dirty diaper. I wanted to sit down and relax after having spent every ounce of consciousness for the previous three hours focused on my child's every need, but then "the boss" would say, "Oh no you don't. I want something else, and I want it now! And by the way, you figure out what it is that I want!" Oh, the joy of parenting infants.

In counseling new parents I often found that this perceived "loss of freedom"—the bondage of parenting—presented great challenges to couples. Partners mourn their loss, but often in private, as they are "supposed" to be so grateful for the blessing of being a parent. This private, and sometimes subconscious, mourning takes the form of depression or aggression. I can recall blaming my wife for this or that until I realized that we *both* were overwhelmed with too much to do and that we *both* were feeling the dense compression and loss of freedom. I also recall the decompression and excited anticipation of "the return of *my* life" when the dust began to settle after two years of infanthood. Then, alas, the decision to have another kid and start the upheaval all over again!

First Child

I'm squishing my feet in the mud with you,
My toes wiggle as your smile breaks through,
And at times I stand, and stuck I am,
Dirt and grime sunshine baby lamb.

REFLECTION ON "FIRST CHILD"

My first child. What an experience. There was little in my life up to that point to prepare me for what was in store for me. The richness, the depth, the intensity. In short order I was in love—all of me. "Oh my God," I would think, "this is amazing." I felt one with Nature. I felt like I had been called off the bench to play in The Game. Invited to advance from pretending or playing on the periphery into the real deal. "Real" is the right word to describe my feelings. The image that came to mind then was a Huck Finn type of image. Sitting on a riverbank, bare feet, squishing my toes in the mud alongside my new best friend. And when my baby Amanda would smile her baby smile, it would break through my cloudy moods like a sunrise.

But there was also the other, negative, side of being a parent of an infant. As I previously mentioned, loss of freedom was a biggie. Couldn't go here and couldn't go there without either considerable planning or the intrusion of a baby. I relinquished most of my recreational and leisure activities for the RESPONSIBILITY of caring for a newborn. It began to feel claustrophobic—trapped by choice in a house filled with crying, poopy diapers, worrying, sleep deprived ... So, at times I felt very "stuck"—like when you get too far into mud and it holds a suction grip on you. That was the feeling. It felt good and bad at the same time. I just felt In Life and In Love and, at times, in a bit of danger!

In the context of a culture that only promotes the blessing and wonder of having children, the reality of having a child was a bit startling. It was difficult to respond to people's gushy sentiments about how wonderful it must be when it was so much more complex than that for me. I cherished the few people who dared to be frank about their experience of parenting, expressing the pluses and the minuses. I'd rather have the whole truth than just a portion.

Since then I have felt bad for the many mothers I counseled who were raised with a two-dimensional Disneyland image of the pure wonder of parenthood. What a cruel twist it is for a new mother, expecting pure joy with her newfound role in life, to experience the negative side of it all. Not feeling instant love but instead a strange aloofness. Feeling the panic of the enormity of responsibility and the unpreparedness for taking it on. Feeling the imprisonment of trying to meet the responsibility. Feeling exhausted. Feeling totally out of control with a colicky baby screaming incessantly. Watching, as if from a distance, their relationship with their spouse (if there was one) disintegrate as they blame each other for not carrying enough of the burden. Watching their fun time together dwindle to almost nothing. Trying to find comfort in handling this bald, drooling, pooping, fragile blob of wriggling flesh. What a mess it can become! What I've just described is not unusual. I'd venture to say it is commonplace.

So, for some of those who buy the "pure joy" story hook, line, and sinker, it can become a very rude awakening. One that comes with heaping doses of guilt. I saw it too often as a therapist in Utah, where the Mormon culture, in its emphasis on family, can sometimes be a purveyor of the myth. The women who experienced the more complex version of things, as described above, just felt horrible about themselves. I could see the weight of the world come off their back as I normalized some of their experience for them.

The cruelest twist I have seen Mother Nature deliver, though, after delivering a healthy baby, is postpartum depression. It stabs right in the heart. It takes every ounce of effort for the mother to just do the basic caretaking—feeding, holding. There's no warmth, no love, coming from within. That's terrifying to a woman—making her wonder if there's something demonic about her—or at least something very, very cold and hard. Like all states of emotion, though, it almost always passes. But, it's a hard journey.

Finally, for me, there was the simple reality that childrearing is hard work, hence the reference in the poem to "dirt and grime." It's the hardest work I have ever done. It's challenging and relentless. You don't get through it without getting dirt under your fingernails.

Dad Hands

Dinosaur Dad hands
Caress the tiny toes
And massage a gentle lullaby,
As the rain outside blows.

REFLECTION ON "DAD HANDS"

This experience poignantly crystallized my awareness of being a protector. Here I was, holding my tiny, helpless baby. We were at peace. All was well and, as if hypnotized by this peace and love, my awareness narrowed. Only my son and me. Together. Then my trance was broken by the gentle sound of the wind blowing rain against the window. I looked up and noticed a storm brewing outside. The juxtaposition of our embracing peace inside the house against the growing storm outside popped out this thought: "I will always protect you to the best of my ability. You can count on it!" I've never been clearer about anything. Though I had no idea what storms would be coming our way, I knew they would show up, and my resolve eviscerated any anxiety. That commitment becomes more complicated as children grow into adulthood and have responsibility for making all sorts of decisions they don't make when they are young children. I have noticed that even when I have thought that the trouble they were experiencing was of their own making, my instinct to protect stayed strong even though less clear. Does a parent stop protecting their child if the child is now an adult—even a 65-year-old adult? Does that protective instinct weaken as an adult child makes poor decisions over and over again? Does it go away if the adult child's behavior has resulted in deep hurt and even harm to the parent? Of course, that protective instinct and commitment varies from parent to parent. I know from my own mother that it can stay firm forever.

Bonding

The sneak bug snuck,
And tucked himself in-
to the fold of my heart,
With his gassy little grin.

REFLECTION ON "BONDING"

Being able to write this poem was a great relief to me. It is written about my second child. I had totally and completely fallen in love with my first child, my daughter. When it came time for our second, I was frightened. I could not conceive of how my heart could allow another child to enter and find any place in there other than a second-class seat. I certainly did not want that to happen. Doomsday scenarios ran through my mind. "This child would never find his rightful share of my love, which would screw him up and would create conflicted relationships throughout the family." I would have dumped sewage in paradise. Me ... and only me ... ruining a perfect thing by trying to stretch for more. My blood ran cold thinking of this.

And my son was not a snuggly "Gerber baby." He was uncomfortable often. He arched his back due to digestive discomfort and he was difficult to comfort. He did not like to be held closely facing my body but preferred to face outward. It was a rough start-up. But I followed an instinct that has shown its value on several occasions in my life—to lean into the storm searching for the center. So, I pushed myself to assume caretaking responsibilities instead of sloughing them off whenever I could. I chose to spend time with him when I could have avoided him. Then, one day, one moment, something clicked.

I was sitting with him in my lap. He was comfortable at last. I was relaxed. Our eyes met. And he smiled. At that moment we bonded. I knew that everything was going to be all right. Thank God. With time I have been amazed at the expandability of love. I actually wonder now if it has any limit.

And, unfortunately, I have also experienced the closing up and hardening of my heart after repeated deep injuries. This is where I find myself after living my life to this point. I miss my more open and softer heart.

Donna

Hearts cascade,
And mountain stars shine,
Magnetized in heaven,
Your soul and mine.

REFLECTION ON "DONNA"

My grandfather was a stoic. He was big and strong. His strength was forged in the cauldrons of immigrating alone to the United States from Russia as a young teenager, of soldiering experiences in the brutal World War I, and of the struggles of the Great Depression. But he knew love and tenderness too. It leapt from his laugh and his sparkling eyes. He had been through a lot, and he knew a lot. And so, I took note when he wrote in a letter to me and my fiancée after our announcement that we would be getting married, "It's a match made in heaven." I thought, "How does he know? We're not around him much. He doesn't have a chance to see us together very often. I don't talk to him much." But he *knew.*

My relationship with my wife has been marked by magic from the beginning. She asked me out on a date when we were teenagers. I wanted to say "No" because I was shy with girls. My mother, however, wanting me to spread my wings socially, said to me, "Go out with her. You're not going to marry her. Just go out with her." And so, I did. We had a fun time together. We subsequently dated for a couple of years, and when a new girl moved in across the street from out of town, I suggested that she and my girlfriend would like each other. The problem, though, was that I became infatuated with the new girl next door. When that happened, and I left town for college, my girlfriend and I broke up. We tried to remain friends, and so we wrote each other letters. When I would return to town, I would see both of them.

Then, one day while at college, I received a letter from her telling me that she still had strong feelings for me and that this attempt to "be friends" was too painful for her. She wished me luck in my life and bade me goodbye. As I was reading this in my dormitory room, I had Bob Dylan's *Nashville Skyline* album playing in the background. And the lyrics of the song playing echoed in my ear as I read and reread the letter: *"If you find someone who gives you all of her love/Take it to your heart, don't let it stray/For one thing's for certain/You'll surely be a-hurtin'/If you throw it all away."* The light snapped on … "This is the person I should be with." And so, the story goes. We have been together ever since. That was 1971!

We have faced our challenges and nearly fallen apart a number of times. But introspection on my relationship with her makes me feel like there's a star above us, sometimes clouded, but ever-present. I feel blessed to have her in my life. I take some credit—but largely feel lucky. This poem echoes my grandfather's insight: "It's a match made in heaven." And, it is a bow of reverence to the mystery of synchronicity. How and why did all of these things come together in a moment to illuminate my soul?

In Love

Your eyes opened wide,
And swallowed mine.
That's fine.
I only need them for you.

REFLECTION ON "IN LOVE"

My best friend has always insisted that monogamy is an unnatural human invention linked with oppression and suppression. He never got married. On the other hand, I got married when I was 22 years old. This poem immediately brings to mind the "wandering eye" phenomenon. Despite my deep love and attraction for and to my wife, my eye has wandered many times, always driven by lust. Further, motivation "to wander" has been fueled by a cultural definition of "studliness," namely sexual conquests. So, I have been in many situations where I wanted to have sex with someone other than my wife and have had the opportunity to act on that desire. For the most part, I have been very loyal. And I have never regretted decisions to be loyal. In retrospect, I have always known that my wife is "the one" for me and that I never want to hurt her or lose her. Sexual satisfaction pales in comparison with relationship satisfaction. And with my wife, I have had both. I have always known it's a stupid calculus to jeopardize that. By constitution I have a good deal of self-restraint. Imagining being eye-to-eye with my wife confronting a transgression of trust has served as a powerful restraint for me. I do not want to be that person who would cut my dearest friend and lover with a switchblade. And, I've been blessed with a good deal of confidence about my personhood, thereby not being compelled to "prove myself" via sexual conquests. Also, maybe due to my shy nature and my very early attachment to my wife when I was 16 years old, I didn't really develop "pursuit skills" to much of a degree in regard to females. And, as has happened so often in my life, I have been blessed with undeserved good luck in not getting caught when I have transgressed. It is this convergence of factors that have protected me from irreparably damaging the most precious aspect of my life.

Together

Cool, moist, green apple skin,
Lies on my soul.
Wispy hair,
You are here.

REFLECTION ON "TOGETHER"

At times my life leaves me feeling like I've been toiling in the hot sun and humid air. I feel hot … weary … grimy. Then it all changes when I snuggle with my wife and we talk little and light. I am so grateful. I feel blessed. My slave-master mind goes on break and lets me go swimming to cool off. To rest. To reconnect with myself. Quiet time. Comforting strokes. Fingers through hair. It's literally a love potion … a comforting balm. I wonder if that's what a baby's experience is when it cries and is comforted with an embrace and soft voice.

And then I think of all the people who do not have that comforting option in their lives, and those who have never experienced that level of comfort with another person. They don't even know it's a possibility in life, something to aspire toward or hope for. The other evening my wife and I were enjoying a cocktail together, with music playing, and preparing something for dinner. We took a moment to appreciate together how much it means to each of us to be able to hang out without pressure or expectation, just enjoying the experience together. As Billy Joel wrote in "Just the Way You Are,"

> I don't want clever conversation,
> I never want to work that hard,
> I just want someone that I can talk to,
> I want you just the way you are.

The Lover

I'm a loner and a lover at heart,
I love being alone with you,
And I love being alone ...
With you.

REFLECTION ON "THE LOVER"

All people have some need for interpersonal intimacy as well as some need for personal space. The balance that defines a person's comfort zone varies from individual to individual. And, for any individual, which of these needs bobs to the surface at any point in time is a complex function of many factors, and therefore less than completely predictable. Consequently, the management of these needs in a relationship can cause considerable tension. Expecting to be "in sync" with your partner is a lot to hope for. This push-pull dynamic is a major process that couples struggle to manage well.

I have commonly observed with myself and others where one party in a relationship is feeling the need for connection when at that same time their partner is wanting some personal space. This situation of conflicting needs gets played out in a number of ways. The best resolution occurs when each party recognizes each of their needs as valid and they negotiate a compromise—for example, "Give me an hour or so to unwind and then let's have dinner together and talk." More commonly, though, each person is too selfishly focused on having their need met, and they don't recognize that it is normal in relationships for needs to not always synchronize. So the one will push for connection by initiating a conversation and the other might go through the motions of listening but will actually not be listening well at all—they want some distance.

The stereotype of this is a partner hiding behind the newspaper or busying themselves with tidying while robotically repeating the mantra of "Yes, honey" as the other person jabbers on and on, trying to connect.

At this juncture the process often becomes really insidious. In response to the feeling or intuition that they are not being listened to, and feeling unloved and unimportant as a result, the talker ups their efforts by *talking more* or *talking more loudly* or by *provoking a reaction*, usually one of anger. The "listener," then, feeling the full-court press, ups their efforts to get away by becoming more aloof, shutting down verbally, getting high or drunk, or simply leaving the scene. Each person's reactions push the other to a more extreme position until a conflict erupts. And, when the arena for this interplay is sex, the whole reaction is hotter, quicker, and usually uglier. One person is in an amorous mood when the other is not. Sexual rejection can stab deeply, resulting in eruption of conflict.

This issue of negotiating closeness and distance is one of the top issues that couples have to deal with. Those who figure it out do well. Others tend to live with more conflict than they want or they grow increasingly distant from one another until the relationship essentially dissolves.

I gave this poem to my wife to let her know how much I appreciated being together in a connected and interactive way and that I also appreciated being in a relationship that respected personal space. I wanted her to know that when I retreated, it was not equivalent to saying "I don't love you anymore"—but instead that I simply wanted alone time. And I wanted her to know that her understanding of this meant a lot to me. Getting good at this dance of connection and disconnection has been critical to our long-standing loving relationship. And, as an aside, it is basically the only dance we know how to do well together.

Lucky

A shooting star came shimmering down,
As I daydreamed on the knoll,
And it, by chance, anointed Me,
Companion of your soul.

REFLECTION ON "LUCKY"

So many good things happen in life when we least expect them. And, so it can be with love. When we are trying hard, it can seem like no one is "the one." But while we are relaxing and doing our thing, it can show up. Someone notices us and likes what they see. That's how I felt about meeting my wife. It happened when I wasn't looking. And my most creative problem solving occurs to me while I'm taking a walk or doing something disconnected from the problem itself. Sometimes it's just best to get at something sideways rather than head-on.

When it comes to love, though, it can be hard to be patient and cool. It can become so desired that it becomes a goal that we attack. I've known people who have checklists of characteristics they are looking for. They take a very "right brain" thing—love—and throw it to the "left brain," the rational, problem-solving one, to figure out. I've never seen it work. Love just has so much mystery to it, which is why it has fascinated artists forever. It's ephemeral. As a psychotherapist, I always found this a difficult topic to be helpful with. Basically, my only insight was the paradoxical one to stop trying so hard. That's not a well-received message when someone is telling you they are starved for love. The best I found I could do was to help them add things to focus on having to do with growing themselves— with becoming themselves more fully. Sometimes this would lead to joining clubs or taking classes to further their own interests, and there, in the context of authentic engagement with an activity, love appeared. In the main, though, I think that anyone who finds true love can feel lucky.

A guiding principle for me in my life has been to do my best to guide myself into activities and relationships that I found engaging, and to minimize relationships and activities that were less so. I have come to trust this process, as it has rewarded me time and again. If I am true to myself, true work, enjoyment, and relationships find their way to me. Truth attracts Truth.

Magic

Love struck strong today,
In the midst of my disarray,
Is it your eyes or your smile...
what exactly do you do?
I think there's something magic going on
with you.

Reflection on "Magic"

My life has lots going on. At least it feels that way. And, while I think I manage it all pretty well, it is not due to my organizational skills. The word "disarray" characterizes my experience more than "array." I'm not one who carries a day/month planner. I don't have well-designed long-term plans. I get up and start doing stuff. I'm more spontaneous than planful in my approach to the big arc of my life, though I'm more disciplined than spontaneous in the small chunks of hours and days. Somehow it works out. I jump around, attending to one thing and then another. I imagine it might feel like being a jazz musician improvising (oh, how I wish I had developed the chops to play jazz). He or she gets started without a note-by-note score, with a general sense of direction, and puts one note after another. At times they must be very pleased with the path they pave and at others less so. Some days I feel like it all came together, and others I feel it was a jumble. And so it goes. I have suggested that my tombstone might say "He did a bunch of stuff and tried hard."

While my life is spinning in my mind and heart, I sometimes feel like a big anchor dropped over my bow and strongly settled in the sand below. It immediately provides a sense of stability in the face of stormy winds and forceful waves. It is love. It comes to me with clarity and power. It is not the lighter feeling of love that comes with play or appreciation. It doesn't come to my mind. It envelops and invades me *for just a moment*. And in that moment my life simplifies and clarifies enormously. It co-occurs with the presence of my wife. I can't pin it down on anything in particular other than being in the same space and breathing the same air as she. A lovely mystery.

Bliss

With anticipation,
My world begins to melt.
Embracing amongst engulfing cushions,
The corporeal blissfully crumbles.

Lust

As you lounge … your feet without
underpants respire,

Your speaking heaves your chest
and fans the fire,

And your robe makes suggestions.

I'm waiting for you to retire.

Skin

Skin on skin,
Wet between,
Poised on a joyful scream.
Suspended in a warm fog.

REFLECTION ON "BLISS" ... "SKIN"

Loving, caring touch is air for the soul. Harry Harlow conducted a series of famous studies of infant rhesus monkeys that demonstrated the importance of maternal touch and comforting in normal development. Monkeys denied adequate touch or comfort, for example those who were raised with a wire surrogate "mother," developed a variety of social inadequacies and emotional problems.

We need human touch. My mother and father had a long-lived love affair. They were soul mates. They adored each other. My mother survived my father's death and after a year or so she revealed to me, "You know what I miss so much? Just touching each other." She missed holding hands. Hugging. Snuggling. It took the wind out of me.

But there's a whole realm of touching that goes far beyond to another basic human need, namely sensual and sexual touch. These poems are about that. They are my personal reflections on skin touching skin, impulsive sex, and lurid lust. These are the responses in youth—of early forays into physical intimacy. Part sensuality, part sexuality, and a pinch of spirituality. I remember well the amazing feeling of cuddling on a couch or in bed, feeling so PURRFECT. It was a feeling of warmth, of connection, of desirability, of release from all care. BLISS. And, often this would become a prelude to sex. So, the feeling state would become decorated with the effervescent energy of anticipation. And then transported to who knows where upon climax. The human experience elevated.

And, then there were the experiences that more rightfully fall into the category of animality—lust. The animal inside would emerge and I would become a predator—albeit a polite one. Relaxing and talking to me after she bathed. Sitting in front of me with just a robe on. Freshly smoothed leg showing from the lower slit in the robe. Half a cleavage showing up top. The clean smells of soap and shampoo. The innocence of a simple conversation. And the feet. I have always been attracted to women's feet. The straight toes, the tender arch, and the strong band of the Achilles. I know I was supposed to be listening. I know we were just talking. But, I really had just one thing on my mind. And I had time. Predator and prey.

Anniversary

A tree swaying in me I see,
With greens and browns and birds that sing.
Breathing in all the history,
I recall ... with awe ... the seedling.

REFLECTION ON "ANNIVERSARY"

I feel so grateful for all the things about my relationship with my wife. Like appreciating a fine painting, or musical composition, or a walk in the woods. You become very sensory—seeing, hearing, feeling, thinking. And, you notice details—the bass line tip-toeing around the melody … the pink paint hidden behind the black in only strategic locations … the dainty wildflowers in the rocky terrain asserting their right-to-be in the harsh wilderness.

There are many times when I watch my wife or simply reflect on our relationship. A smile comes to my face when I see her do little ordinary things—like watch a movie, or sleep, or do the crossword puzzle wearing my glasses. And my heart warms when I reflect on her love and devotion and her giant, radiant smile. And, at anniversary times, I think of all the work—the constant nurturing day in and day out—that a relationship takes. The work of enduring someone's accusations and moods. The work of remaining faithful. The work of being considerate. The work of hanging in there when the waters are rough and your self-interested, pleasure-based instincts tell you to bail. The work of admitting all your failings in the aforementioned realms, becoming vulnerable with oneself and the other.

Then, one day you wake up and the relationship has grown—the irritations are less irritating, the pleasures are warm instead of hot, trust and loyalty buffer suspicion, and friendship has deepened with the sharing of more life experiences. The awe I can feel at these times reminds me of the awe I have in the woods or a forest seeing huge trees and growing seedlings mixed amongst each other, highlighting the perspective of how much goes in to growing over time. Time, endurance, and the sheer will of life inspire awe in me. Like seeing a tiny fragile wildflower amidst a rock outcropping on top of a sparse and harsh mountaintop. As much as I am not a celebration guy, I am grateful for markers that compel reflection.

EPILOGUE

Being

You won't confine me
To what you want to see,
I'll shine until I die,
And blind your tiny eye.

ABOUT THE AUTHOR

Dr. Mayerson is a clinical psychologist who had a private psychotherapy practice for twenty years and he has played an early and ongoing role in developing the field of positive psychology by creating the nonprofit organization VIA Institute on Character to understand scientifically what's best about human beings and how we use those characteristics to build good lives for ourselves and others. Millions of people worldwide take the VIA Survey each year to discover their strengths of character and put them to good use in their lives. His creative spirit has also led to the creation of a number of other nonprofit organizations, the creation of the first online personal health coaching service, the writing/recording/performing of original music, producing the award-winning musical tribute to legendary King Records called *Hidden Treasures: Cincinnati's Tribute to King Records' Legacy*, the introduction of hand sanitizer as a consumer product category, and a patented online group conversation technology. Additionally, he is a businessman and entrepreneur as well as a philanthropist. He derives great satisfaction from playing tennis, listening to music, viewing art, having a good heartfelt conversation, helping others find their time in the light, and precious time with his wife, children, and dog.

Made in the USA
Coppell, TX
13 November 2020

41245652R00142